WATERSIDE WALKS
In Cheshire

James F. Edwards

First published 1999
© James F. Edwards 1999
Reprinted 2004
Revised and updated 2008

COUNTRYSIDE BOOKS
3 Catherine Road
Newbury, Berkshire

ISBN 978 1 85306 556 9

Designed by Graham Whiteman
Maps and photographs by the author

Produced through MRM Associates Ltd., Reading
Printed by Cambridge University Press

*All material for the manufacture of this book
was sourced from sustainable forests.*

This book is dedicated to the waterway engineers of yesteryear – whose hard toil and ingenuity have resulted in a modern-day leisure amenity they could never have imagined.

It is also dedicated to the memory of my late mother, Jean, who is greatly missed.

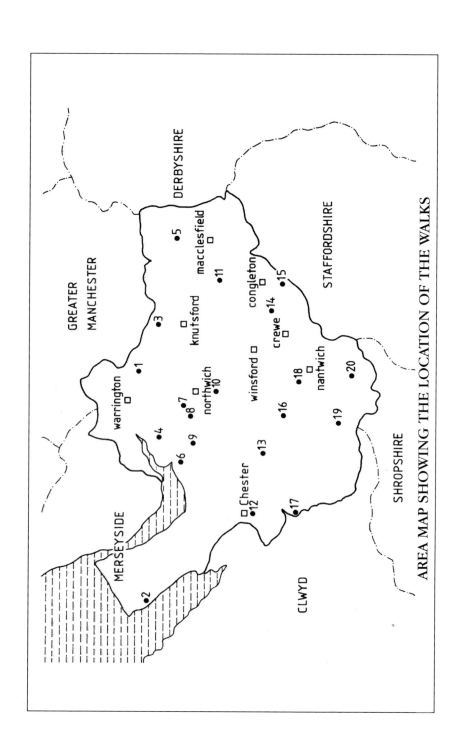

AREA MAP SHOWING THE LOCATION OF THE WALKS

Contents

Introduction   7

Walk

1   Lymm and the Bridgewater Canal *(6 miles)*   11

2   Thurstaston and the Dee Estuary *(4½ miles)*   17

3   Ashley and the Bollin Valley *(7 miles)*   22

4   Daresbury and Two Canals *(6½ miles)*   29

5   Adlington and the Macclesfield Canal *(6½ miles)*   35

6   The River Weaver at Frodsham Bridge *(4¼ miles)*   41

7   Little Leigh and the Weaver Valley: 47
    By River and Canal *(5 miles)*

8   Acton Bridge and the River Weaver *(6 miles)*   52

9   The Weaver Valley at Kingsley *(5 miles)*   57

10 Along the Weaver at Vale Royal *(6½ miles)*   62

11 Redes Mere and Other Lakes *(3½ miles)*   68

12 Chester and the River Dee *(5½ or 7½ miles)*   74

Walk

13 Beeston and the Shropshire Union Canal *(7 miles)*   81

14 The Trent and Mersey Canal at Hassall Green *(4 miles)*   87

15 Mow Cop and the Macclesfield Canal *(5 miles)*   92

16 The Shropshire Union Canal at Barbridge *(8 miles)*   98

17 Farndon and the River Dee *(5 miles)*   104

18 Acton and the 'Shroppie' *(5½ miles)*   110

19 The Shropshire Union Canal at Wrenbury *(5½ miles)*   115

20 The Weaver Valley at Hankelow: Along the Shropshire Union Canal *(4½ miles)*   121

PUBLISHER'S NOTE

We hope that you obtain considerable enjoyment from this book; great care has been taken in its preparation. Although at the time of publication all routes followed public rights of way or permitted paths, diversion orders can be made and permissions withdrawn.

We cannot of course be held responsible for such diversion orders and any inaccuracies in the text which result from these or any changes to the routes nor any damage which might result from walkers trespassing on private property. We are anxious though that all details covering the walks are kept up to date and would therefore welcome information from readers which would be relevant to future editions.

INTRODUCTION

For the walker, there are many delights to be found in the attraction of waterways. Wild flowers and trees usually grow in abundance and there is a profusion of wildlife – especially water-loving birds such as coots, moorhens, herons, grebe and the occasional kingfisher. Walking beside waterways is usually more relaxing than, say, hill-walking because of the obvious absence of changes in elevation; also, gently flowing water has a stimulating and therapeutic effect on those strolling by it. Mixed in with the obvious physical attractions of waterways is also the sense of history associated with them and it adds to the enjoyment of a walk to know something about their development.

Cheshire is fortunate in that, for such a small county, it possesses a wide variety of waterways including rivers, meres and canals. Pride of place must go to the river Weaver, for the whole of its 53 mile course is within the boundary of the county. It rises in the Peckforton Hills, flows south at first towards Audlem, then turns north and passes through Nantwich, Winsford and Northwich to enter the Mersey close to Frodsham. Records show that the river was navigable during medieval times from Frodsham to Northwich. It has played an important part in the economic development of the county since 1763 when the Weaver Navigation from Winsford to Frodsham Bridge was completed which allowed quite large vessels to penetrate its inland reaches. The main cargo transported along its course was salt and the river was connected with 'inland' Britain via the massive Anderton boat lift, near Northwich, which links it with the Trent and Mersey Canal.

The path along the riverside between Winsford and Frodsham Bridge takes the walker through some delightful scenery and the five walks along the Weaver described in this book focus on this stretch of the river.

Another of Cheshire's well-known rivers is the Dee, which flows out of Bala Lake then heads north-eastwards to Corwen, then eastwards through Llangollen and Overton, where it turns northwards. The river then passes through Holt and reaches Chester, at which point it turns north-westwards then broadens into a wide estuary which separates Flintshire from the Wirral. For some of its course the river Dee forms the boundary between England and Wales and its total length is about 80 miles.

Three contrasting walks give a taste of the river: one at Farndon at a point where the Dee forms the border between England and Wales; another at Chester – where there is also an opportunity to circumnavigate the city walls; and finally, a stroll by the estuary between Caldy and Thurstaston on the Wirral Peninsula. Cheshire has numerous other rivers of course and one of these, the Bollin, provides the basis of an interesting excursion from Ashley in the north of the county.

A distinctive feature of the Cheshire countryside is the number of lakes or 'meres' which are to be found in abundance throughout the county. Most of these were formed by glaciation, as at Redes Mere, near Siddington, where yachtsmen, fishermen and walkers can thoroughly enjoy a tranquil and absorbing environment.

Although rivers were, and still are, used for the transport of goods, there were many places which could not be reached and hence the construction of inland canals began, eventually resulting in an extensive network throughout the county. The first English canal to be built entirely independent of rivers was the Bridgewater Canal which was completed in 1763 and initially ran from Worsley to Manchester. The canal was later extended to join the Mersey Estuary at Runcorn and was also linked to the Trent and Mersey Canal at Preston Brook. From Preston Brook, the Trent and Mersey Canal runs south past Northwich to Middlewich and then past Alsager, after which it enters Staffordshire near Kidsgrove where it is joined by the Macclesfield Canal. From Kidsgrove, the Macclesfield Canal runs northwards past Congleton, Macclesfield and Bollington to join the Peak Forest Canal at Marple. A major link in the Cheshire network is the Shropshire Union Canal. Affectionately known as the 'Shroppie', the canal links Ellesmere Port with Wolverhampton, where it joins the Staffordshire and Worcestershire Canal. From Ellesmere Port, the canal passes through Chester – where there is a connection with the river Dee, after which it goes through Nantwich and Audlem – at which point it enters Shropshire. The canal has two important branch lines which are less than 2 miles apart to the north of Nantwich. One of these branches goes to Llangollen, the other goes to Middlewich.

The canals which criss-cross Cheshire are a legacy left by a number of very talented engineers and astute businessmen – without whom we would not possess such an attractive series of waterways. Try to imagine, as you walk along their picturesque routes, the sheer toil and sweat which must have gone into their construction.

Apart from the waterways, the circular routes described in the book take you to some of Cheshire's more interesting villages. The roots of the majority of Cheshire's villages were set down hundreds of years ago at a time when communication was in its infancy. Villagers rarely travelled more than a few miles from their homes with the result that villages and hamlets retained a certain amount of individuality. Hence, there are always different types of architecture and settings to observe when passing through a particular village, for each has its own innate character.

The life blood of any village is its inhabitants, and Cheshire has an abundance of village folk who are fiercely proud of their heritage and really care for their environment. Therefore, readers are asked to respect the villagers' way of life and to use the utmost discretion when parking vehicles. Car parking locations are indicated in the text – but if they are full, or for some reason unusable, please ensure that you park your vehicle in such a way as not to be a nuisance to those who live close by. Many of the walks commence from the village inn where, it must be stressed, parking is only for patrons (the landlords have agreed that vehicles can remain parked whilst patrons complete their walks).

Cheshire is also fortunate in that, apart from its picturesque waterways and villages, it has an abundance of quiet, virtually traffic-free lanes. Many of these lanes have been used in the walks described in this book, not just as interconnecting links between footpaths, but in their own right, as a pleasant part of an overall circular route designed to give the participants variety during their jaunts in the countryside.

Points of interest relating to attractions within striking distance of each individual walk are included with each walk description. The time span covered by these goes from the Roman remains at Chester and the medieval ruins of Beeston Castle, through the splendid Halls of Arley, Tatton, and Capesthorne and the Industrial Revolution at Quarry Bank Mill to the 20th-century motor museum at Mouldsworth. Although an entrance charge is payable for many of the attractions, you learn so much about the county and its history by visiting them.

Places where food and drink can be obtained are also given for each walk. Opening times have not always been included due to the fact that they can often change. However, these can be obtained by using the telephone number which is given at the end of each description. Also, where the menu is the subject of constant variation, only an outline of the type of food available is given. Again, each place can be contacted in order to obtain specific menu details.

What you put on your feet is important. Waterproof walking shoes or boots are recommended, preferably worn over woollen socks. Smooth-soled shoes should not be worn as they can cause accidents and make walking hard work, especially after wet weather. Lightweight waterproof clothing should always be carried to combat the variable English weather. A small rucksack can be useful for carrying such items as food, cameras, binoculars and the like, which help to make a walk that much more enjoyable.

A prime objective has been to provide direct, no-nonsense route descriptions for each walk, coupled with a clear accompanying sketch map. For those requiring more detail, the relevant OS Landranger 1:50 000 map numbers are given.

Do not be afraid to venture out during the winter months, for an excursion on a cold, clear day when frost has hardened the ground underfoot can be most rewarding, especially when coupled with a warming drink and a hearty meal taken in pleasant surroundings. However, if you wish to enjoy the facilities of an inn following the completion of a walk please remember to leave muddy walking boots in your car.

Finally, some words of thanks. As with previous surveys I have been accompanied during the preparations for this book by my mother who was an excellent walking companion and had a discerning eye which brought to my attention many things I would otherwise have missed. For her helpful comments and suggestions, I am most grateful. The task of deciphering my handwriting and converting it into a typed manuscript was expertly carried out by Tracy Atkinson. I must also thank all the managers of the various inns, restaurants and tea-shops for taking time from their busy schedules in order to answer my many questions. And last, but by no means least, I met some extremely kind and interesting folk – the inhabitants of Cheshire.

James F. Edwards

LYMM AND THE BRIDGEWATER CANAL

This walk takes you alongside a variety of waterways, combining paths, tracks and country lanes to produce a most rewarding excursion into the attractive countryside of north Cheshire.

Lymm Dam

Lymm is a delightful place with much to interest the inquiring visitor. The village is built on a natural outcrop of sandstone rock out of which the streets have been cut. Part of the rock was utilised during the construction of the village's best-known landmark, the ancient cross located at its heart. About 1770 the Bridgewater Canal was extended from Worsley to Runcorn, cutting through the village. The canal brought benefits in the form of quicker and cheaper transport, thus boosting local industries. From Lymm, the canal runs through Grappenhall to enter the Mersey through a series of locks at Runcorn. A short stroll around the village reveals many appealing buildings, half-timbered houses, interesting shops and five inns!

11

Apart from the Bridgewater Canal, Lymm has other watery ingredients; a large dam is nearby – the outfall from which flows through the village centre – and there are numerous streams and ponds in the vicinity.

The Golden Fleece inn, which is close to the centre of the village near to the bridge which crosses the canal at the end of the walk, is a good source of refreshment. Food is served every lunchtime and in the evening with a selection of roast joints being an additional attraction every Sunday lunchtime. The menu offers a wide choice for every course. The Village Bar, which is at street level, was once the village cobbler's shop, but is now used as a dining area. The inn boasts a splendid canalside beer garden with a separate play area for children. Telephone: 01925 755538.

- HOW TO GET THERE: The A56 connects Altrincham with the outskirts of Warrington. Lymm is situated between these two places, the village centre lying just to the north of the A56.
- PARKING: There is a public car park off Pepper Street, not far from Lymm Cross – an ancient stone edifice in the centre of the village. Alternatively, if you are using the facilities of the Golden Fleece inn, you may park there.
- LENGTH OF THE WALK: 6 miles. Map: OS Landranger 109 Manchester (GR 684873).

THE WALK

1. On leaving the car park in Pepper Street, pass the ancient cross and turn left. The road turns and is carried over a stream, where there is a weir on the left. Immediately turn left now, to enter The Dingle, and pass cottages to follow a macadam path through trees, which keeps parallel with the stream on the left. After 250 yards climb up a flight of steps to arrive at a crossing road. Walk straight across the road, taking care, to follow a well-trodden path which follows the edge of Lymm Dam, where a sign points to Crosfield Bridge and The Bongs.

There is a most attractive view across the waters of the dam at this point where St Mary's church can be seen.

Follow the 'Easy Access trail' which climbs to the right and then follow a well-defined path which generally stays parallel with the dam. Pass over a fenced-in wooden footbridge close by the waterside and keep on to follow the footpath through trees. Keep forward in

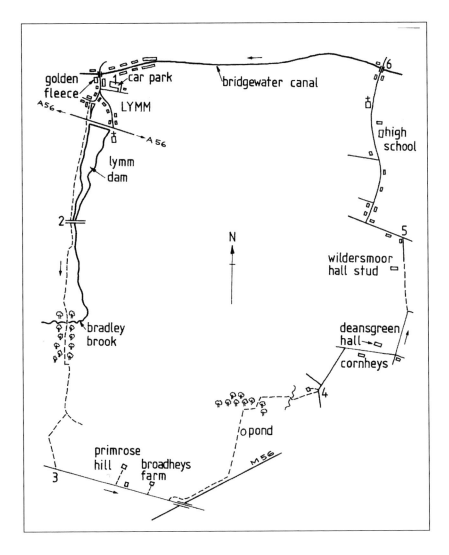

the direction of Crosfield Bridge and pass over a short, fenced-in, wooden bridge. A well-defined path takes you to a large, balustraded, stone bridge.

2. Do not cross the bridge, but keep forward in the direction of The Bongs to descend steps. The path turns to right and left shortly, over a stream. There is a fork now. Keep to the right here, to follow a hedged-in path where there is a field on the right. Pass sunken ponds and then

13

Lymm Cross in the centre of the village.

arrive at a wooded valley which is known as The Bongs. Descend steps and cross Bradley Brook via a plank-bridge, and then climb out of the valley up a flight of steps. Keep on, along a straight length of fenced-in path through woodland. Where the path turns to the left at a facing hedgerow follow it and then go over a stile to enter a large field. Keep along the left hand side of the field, where there is a ditch, and a hedgerow, on the immediate left. Go over a stile at the field corner which is set at the side of a gate and enter a hedged-in track. After only 30 yards, leave the track to the right, over a stile. Keep on, across the next field to a stile which can be seen in a crossing hedgerow about 200 yards away. Go over the stile to follow a well-defined path which takes you up the next field to a stile in a crossing hedgerow which is about 200 yards away. Go over the stile to arrive at a crossing road.

3. Turn left and follow the roadside pavement. Pass Primrose Hill Nurseries and the entrance drive of Broadheys Farm to arrive at a bridge which carries the road over the M56 motorway. Turn left here, before the bridge, to go through a gap at the side of a gate. Follow a fenced-in macadam drive which runs parallel with the motorway. The drive finishes at a facing gate. Go over a stile on the right here, and keep forward in the same direction as before, to follow the edge of a

14

large field, keeping a fence (and the motorway) on your immediate right.

After 250 yards, and where there is a footpath sign, turn left. With the fence at your back, bear slightly right to follow a path across the field in the direction of trees which can be seen about ¼ mile away. About two thirds of the way across the field there is a sunken pond a few yards away on the right. Arrive in front of the trees. Turn right here, to follow the field edge, with the trees now on your immediate left. Go over a fence-stile at the field corner and bear left to follow a path through trees and undergrowth. After only 80 yards, go over another stile to enter a large field. With the stile at your back, walk forward across the field towards a farm which can be seen, about ¼ mile away, straight ahead. A stile comes into view in a crossing hedgerow. Go over the stile and cross a stream to enter another field. Straight ahead, a dwelling can be seen. Walk towards the right hand side of the dwelling and pass to the right of its garden hedgerow to arrive at a stile at the field corner. Go over the stile and join a lane close by the entrance drive which leads to the dwelling.

4. Turn left along the lane and almost immediately pass a narrow lane which goes off to the left. After ¼ mile arrive at a T-junction. Turn right here. The lane takes you past a dwelling called Cornheys. A little further on, the imposing Georgian building of Deansgreen Hall can be seen, half-hidden by trees, over to the left. Arrive at a staggered junction of lanes where there is a post-box set in a brick post. Turn left here to follow Kay Lane. After a straight ¼ mile the lane turns sharply to the right. Leave the lane to the left here, to enter a grassy track which is hedged-in. The track leads to a gate. Pass through a gap at the side of the gate. On the left now is Wildersmoor Hall Stud. The track becomes a macadam lane a little further on, and leads to a crossing road.

5. Cross the road, taking care, and turn left to follow the roadside pavement. After 180 yards turn right to enter Oughtrington Lane. Keep along the laneside pavement and pass Foxley Close and Longbutt Lane. Keep on, past Lymm High School and then gradually descend past the church of St Peter. At the bottom of the descent arrive at a bridge which carries the lane over the Bridgewater Canal. Walk over the bridge and turn left to join the canal towpath.

6. Turn right along the towpath to stroll away from the bridge you have just walked over.

You are now walking alongside an extension of the famous canal which ushered in the canal age and, with it, the Industrial Revolution in Britain. The Bridgewater Canal was engineered by James Brindley to distribute coal from the Duke of Bridgewater's estates at Worsley on the outskirts of Manchester.

Keep on, along the towpath, and shortly after passing Lymm Cruising Club, leave the canal to the right, just before a bridge is reached. Walk over the bridge to arrive back in the centre of Lymm.

PLACES OF INTEREST

About 5 miles due south of Lymm, and accessible via the A56, B5159 and an unclassified road between High Legh and Great Budworth, are *Arley Hall and Gardens*. The Hall is a fine example of early Victorian 'Jacobean' style and is surrounded by 12 acres of beautiful gardens. Apart from the Hall and gardens there is a chapel, a gift shop and a restaurant. The gardens are normally open during the afternoon between April and September (closed on Mondays) but the opening times for the Hall vary. Telephone: 01565 777353.

THURSTASTON AND THE DEE ESTUARY

The walk takes you to the top of Thurstaston Hill with its magnificent vistas and then descends to cross fields before passing through the leafy suburbs of the village of Caldy. The return leg of the walk takes in a section of the Wirral Way by the shores of the Dee Estuary before returning to Thurstaston along a country lane.

The Dee Estuary

Thurstaston can boast one of the most attractive beauty spots on the Wirral Peninsula. Thurstaston Hill is a vantage point for magnificent views across the Dee Estuary to Wales – together with vistas across the Wirral towards Liverpool and beyond. The village possesses a hall, the history of which dates back to the Norman Conquest when Hugh Lupus, nephew of William the Conqueror, was the first Norman Earl of Chester. Another attraction of the area is the Wirral Country Park, where a linear footpath keeps close to the shores of the Dee Estuary along the route of a now defunct railway line which once connected West Kirby with Hooton.

The Cottage Loaf inn in Thurstaston is a large, friendly establishment with a host of exposed beams, brickwork and open fireplaces. Meals are served during the week from 12 noon to 2 pm and 6 pm to 9 pm. At weekends meals are available continuously between 12 noon and 9 pm. A wide choice of food is on offer and there is a traditional menu as well as daily specials. At weekends roast joints are a speciality. A Whitbread house, the inn provides a large selection of beers, cask ales and draught lagers. Telephone: 0151 648 2837.

- HOW TO GET THERE: The A540 connects Chester with Heswall, West Kirby and Hoylake on the Wirral Peninsula. The tiny village of Thurstaston lies just off this road midway between Heswall and West Kirby. The A540 is easily reached from junction 4 of the M53 motorway – via the A5137 through Brimstage to Heswall.
- PARKING: The Cottage Loaf inn fronts onto the A540 at Thurstaston. About 250 yards past the inn, in the direction of West Kirby, there is a roadside car park at Thurstaston Common.

  Alternatively, there is a car park at Caldy – which is reached via the B5140 – which intersects the A540 about a mile from Thurstaston. To reach this car park enter Croft Drive, which commences opposite the village church, and follow it as it turns next right. After ¼ mile, arrive at Wirral Country Park car park, which is on the right (GR 223850). You would then start the walk at point 5.
- LENGTH OF THE WALK: 4½ miles. Map: OS Landranger 108 Liverpool (GR 244847).

THE WALK

1. On leaving the car park at Thurstaston Common, follow the roadside pavement in the direction of the Cottage Loaf inn. After 150 yards turn left to go through a kissing-gate where a sign points towards Royden Park. A well-defined path takes you through trees and then past a school. Turn left now to climb along a path over open slabs of sandstone rock. Arrive at the triangulation point on the top of Thurstaston Hill.

The views from here are superb and a nearby plinth has all the surrounding landmarks etched into a display plate.

2. Having absorbed all the views, descend to the right away from the

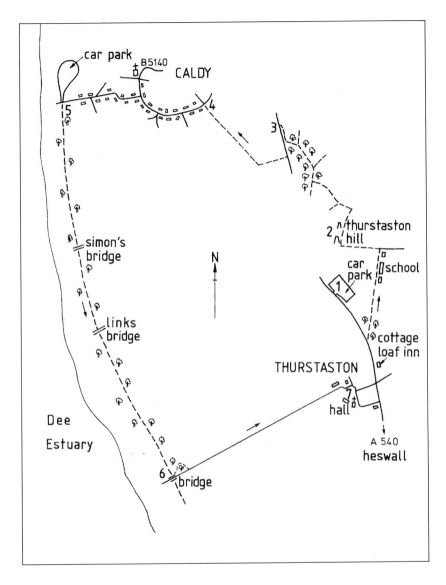

display plinth over open slabs of sandstone rock. About 100 yards from the plinth there is a path which begins on the left between two seats which are about 15 yards apart. After only 5 yards, the path forks. Take the right fork and descend through heather to arrive at a crossing path. Turn right and follow the main path. The path hugs trees on the left shortly. Arrive at a fork. Take the left fork and follow the main path

On top of Thurstaston Hill.

as it descends through trees. At the bottom of the descent there are tall shrubs of gorse. The path turns to the right at a facing wall. The path hugs the wall and leads to a crossing road which is accessed through a gap in the wall.

3. Cross the road, taking care, and turn left to follow the roadside pavement. After only 80 yards leave the pavement, to the right, through a wooden kissing-gate. Follow the edge of a field now, keeping a hedgerow on your immediate right. Go through a metal kissing-gate at the field corner and turn right to follow a path between fences. Pass over a stile and keep on, in the same direction as before, to follow a track between fences. The track leads to a crossing road opposite Long Hey Road.

4. Turn left past house number 19 and follow the roadside pavement. These are the leafy suburbs of the village of Caldy where there are many large, attractive dwellings.

Keep on past Links Hey Road and Barton Hey Drive and turn next left into Croft Drive. Shortly after passing Croft Drive West and the other end of Barton Hey Drive you arrive at the Wirral Way. (The alternative parking location, the Wirral Country Park car park, is on the right here.)

5. Turn left opposite the car park entrance and join the linear footpath known as the Wirral Way. This follows the route of the old railway line between West Kirby and Hooton. The last passenger to travel by train along the old railway line was in fact the Queen (in 1957).

The raised embankment is a fine platform for long views across the Dee Estuary to Wales. Pass under Simon's Bridge and Links Bridge.

6. At the next bridge (Station Road Bridge) leave the linear footpath up steps on the left. Follow a path which winds through trees for a short distance and then join a path, where the way is right. Arrive at a crossing lane.

The way is to the left to follow the laneside pavement; however, for an excellent view across the Dee Estuary, turn right to walk over the bridge.

To continue, follow the lane as directed. The spire of Thurstaston church can be seen straight ahead. After a straight ½ mile the lane winds and takes you past the Old School House and Dawpool Farm. Follow the lane as it turns to the right and keep on past a road which climbs to the left.

7. On the right now, across a green, can be seen Thurstaston Hall and to its left the parish church. Follow the lane past the church and turn left to climb past Church Farm. Arrive at a crossing road. Turn left here and keep along the roadside pavement. Pass Station Road and turn right to cross to the other side of the road, taking care. Walk past the Cottage Loaf inn to arrive back at Thurstaston Common car park.

PLACES OF INTEREST

About 8 miles by road to the south-east of Thurstaston, and accessible via the A540 and B5134 through Neston, are the extensive 62 acre *Ness Gardens* which are a delight throughout all the seasons of the year. Telephone: 0151 353 0123.

ASHLEY AND THE BOLLIN VALLEY

The outward leg of the walk takes you into the Bollin valley and follows the course of the river to Castle Mill. On the return journey some lush, green Cheshire pastures are crossed by way of paths, tracks and lanes.

The Bollin valley near Castle Mill.

A tiny village at the edge of the conurbation of Greater Manchester, Ashley has a post office, a church, a cricket pitch and a village pub. The surrounding area contains many scenic footpaths and popular beauty spots. One of the main attractions of the area is the river Bollin, whose waters flow peacefully through a wooded valley where wildlife abounds. The river winds its way around the outskirts of Hale and Bowdon after which it passes under the Bridgewater Canal at Bollington prior to entering the Manchester Ship Canal near Warburton. Between Ashley and the Bollin there are many old farms and dwellings where life goes on much as it has over many long years.

The Greyhound dates from the 18th century and is actually quite a bit larger than it appears. Originally called the Orrell Arms, the pub took its present name in 1841, when it became part of the Tatton Estate. Owned by Greenalls, this attractive inn serves a wide variety of food at lunchtime and in the evening every day of the week. Daily choices are displayed on a chalkboard in the lounge area. During summertime there is a beer garden. Telephone: 0161 941 2246.

- HOW TO GET THERE: Ashley is situated on a minor road midway between the A538 and A556, 2 miles to the south of Hale. Access can be gained from either junction 6 or 7 of the M56 motorway.
- PARKING: There is a car park at the Greyhound Inn (for patrons). Alternatively, there is a parking layby at Castle Hill, by the road which connects Ashley with the A538 about ½ mile from where the A538 passes under the main runway of Manchester Airport (GR 802837). You would then start the walk at point 4.
- LENGTH OF THE WALK: 7 miles. Map: OS Landranger 109 Manchester (GR 775843).

THE WALK

1. From the Greyhound Inn, enter the facing Back Lane, in the direction of Ringway and Wilmslow, and follow the laneside pavement past Ashley Primary School, keeping on past a lane which goes off to the right. At the junction with Castle Mill Lane, turn left in the direction of Hale and Altrincham. Follow the laneside pavement and cross the M56 motorway. Leave the lane to the right now, over a stile, where a footpath sign points to Bankhall Lane and Ross Mill. Keep along a field edge where there is a fence and hedgerow on your immediate right. Go over a stile at the field corner and follow the edge of the next field to where, after 100 yards, there is a stile on the right. Cross the stile and turn left to follow an obvious path which winds through a wood, where the waters of the river Bollin can be seen down on the right. A substantial footbridge gives access to the opposite side of the river.

2. Immediately on crossing the footbridge turn right to follow a well-defined path which stays close to the river for a few yards, and then bears to the left and takes you over a metal bridge. Climb and then keep right at a junction of ways to quickly reach level ground on the edge of a golf course. Follow a track which hugs the edge of trees on the left here, around the perimeter of the golf course. Enter a hedged-

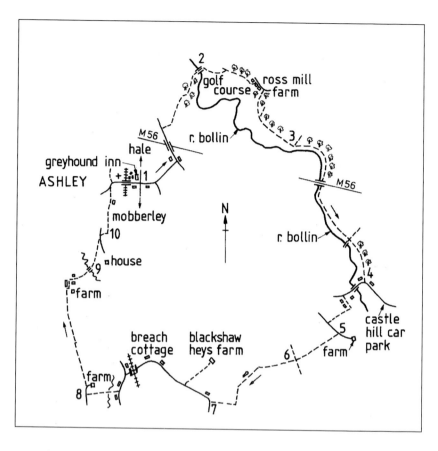

in path now and follow it, as it turns to the left between dwellings, to a crossing lane. Turn right along the lane and pass a converted barn. About 150 yards further on, turn right through a gap in a fence. After only 50 yards there is a junction of ways which both lead to the same place close to where there is a joining path from the right. There is a grassy common here and the path follows its left hand side. The path becomes a rough track and descends, through trees, to more level terrain. Follow the main track and arrive at a junction of ways in front of an old gateway.

3. Keep forward through the gateway to join a path which takes you alongside the river Bollin. Go over a stile and pass under a bridge which carries the M56 motorway over the river. Cross another stile and then enter a field to continue along a riverside path. Go over a plank-

bridge and keep on to follow an obvious path through a rough field. Pass over a stile in a crossing fence and after a further 80 yards go over another stile. There is a junction of paths here and a footbridge spanning the river on the right. Keep forward here, in the same general direction as before, to follow an obvious path which is not as close to the water's edge as before. Descend a short flight of steps and cross a plank-bridge. Keep forward; there are trees on the left now and dwellings come into view straight ahead. The path bears slightly to the right shortly, and leads to a stile at the side of a gate close by a dwelling. Go over the stile and follow a short length of track to arrive at a crossing road.

4. Turn right along the road. (Note: If you are commencing the walk from the car park at Castle Hill, this is the point at which you will join the route. From the car park turn left and descend along the road to where, after 400 yards, you arrive at this point.) Pass a dwelling called Castle Mill and follow the road across the Bollin via a stone bridge. Climb along the roadside but, immediately on passing the entrance to One Castle Mill, leave the road to the left, to enter a track, where a footpath sign points to Morley and Wilmslow. After about 50 yards, keep to the left of a facing gate to go over a step-stile. A narrow path follows the perimeter of a property on the right. Pass over a plank-bridge and stile to enter a large, sloping field. Turn right and gradually climb along the field edge. Go over a stile at the field corner to enter a crossing lane, where the way is left. The lane gently bears to the left and leads towards a farm. On the right here there is a double field gate with stiles at both sides. Cross the right hand stile to enter the field.

5. Navigational care is now required. With the stile at your back there is a pylon in the far distance and this is your aiming point. After 220 yards, pass an isolated stile which is situated between a tree and a telegraph pole. Aim to the right of the pylon now and then go over a stile about 25 yards to its right at the field corner. Keep on, in the same direction as before, to follow a field edge, keeping a hedgerow on your immediate right. After 80 yards there is a junction of paths.

6. Stay along the field edge here, still with the hedgerow on your immediate right, to arrive at a gateway and an old stile. Pass through the gateway – there is a dyke on the left here – to follow a well-

defined path across the next field in the same general direction as before. After 200 yards pass over a stile where there is a small pond on the left. Bear left now and cross the next field, passing to the left of a choked-up pond. Go over a stile near the field corner and walk straight up the centre of the next field. On reaching the end of the field turn right at a facing fence and then go over a stile at the field corner.

Across the next field, over to the right, there is a brick building. Aim well to the left of this and cross the field to pass through a gateway which takes you onto a lane.

7. Turn right along the lane. Pass a dwelling on the right and keep on past the entrance to Blackshaw Heys Farm. Shortly after passing Breach Cottage walk under a bridge which carries the railway over the lane. Arrive at a junction. Turn left here to follow a lane. After 150 yards pass Brook House and then, 50 yards further on, and before the next dwelling is reached, leave the lane to the right via a stile at the side of a gate. Descend along a field edge and after only 30 yards go over a footbridge to traverse Mobberley Brook. Climb up the facing field and then follow level terrain to go over a stile at the left hand side of a large tree. A farm can now be seen across the fields ahead. Follow the left hand edge of a field then pass over a stile to enter a lane.

8. Turn right along the lane. The lane turns right into a farm shortly, but keep forward here, over a stile at the left hand side of a gate. Pass to the right of a large barn and go over two stiles at the side of gates. Follow the right hand edge of a rough field, where there is a hedgerow on the immediate right. Go over a stile and keep along the edge of the next two fields and pass over a further two stiles. Only 20 yards further on, go over a stile on the right to continue, in the same direction as before, along the edge of a large field, but with a hedgerow now on your immediate left. A farm can be seen at the end of the field. Pass over a stile which is close to the garden hedgerow of the farm and turn right and then left to skirt the edge of the farmyard. There is a single storey brick building on the left now. Where this finishes turn right and walk between outbuildings on the right and a large barn on the left. Go over a facing stile and descend along the edge of a field keeping a fence on the right. Bear left shortly to pass over Mobberley Brook via a substantial footbridge.

9. Cross an undulating field to climb to a stile which can be seen, set

The pub at the start of the walk.

in a fence, about 130 yards away. Go over the stile. There is a large, attractive, Georgian style dwelling over to the right here, but bear slightly left now to cross the facing field in the direction of a much smaller dwelling which can be seen between trees, about ¼ mile away. The path converges with a fence and leads to a lane, where the way is left. The lane takes you over a stream. Only 40 yards after joining the lane, leave it to the right, over a stile. Climb up a banking and turn right to follow a field edge. After about 100 yards arrive at a crossing path.

10. Turn left to cross the field where a well-defined path takes you to the right of a telegraph pole which can be seen ahead. About 90 yards after passing the telegraph pole arrive at a stile in a crossing hedgerow. Walk forward now, in the direction of Ashley Cricket Club clubhouse, which can be seen about 300 yards away, straight ahead. Cross two further stiles and arrive on a track to the left of the clubhouse. A short length of facing track leads to a crossing road where the way is right. Follow the roadside pavement and keep on past the church then go over the railway.

A few more strides take you back into the centre of Ashley.

Red deer in Tatton Park

PLACES OF INTEREST

The great park at *Tatton,* which is to the south-west of Ashley, gives a glimpse of a way of life which is hundreds of years old and contains a mansion and hall, a working farm and delightful gardens. Telephone: 01625 534400. Four miles to the east of Ashley, and to the north of Wilmslow, is the award winning museum at *Quarry Bank Mill,* where a 200 year old working environment has been recreated. Telephone: 01625 527468.

DARESBURY AND TWO CANALS

Having explored this fascinating village with its Lewis Carroll connections, the walk takes you across fields to the village of Preston-on-the-Hill, and then onto the towpath of the Bridgewater Canal, via the Trent and Mersey. A 3 mile stroll alongside the canal leads to a gentle climb along Hobb Lane, after which field paths and tracks take you back to Daresbury.

The junction of the Bridgewater and Trent and Mersey Canals.

Visitors come from all over the world to Daresbury. The reason for their pilgrimage is that Lewis Carroll, the author of *Alice's Adventures in Wonderland*, was born here, and all over the village there are reminders of the colourful characters depicted in his stories. Close by the Ring O'Bells inn is the Lewis Carroll Centre, which is housed in the former Sessions House which, together with an adjoining barn, has been restored to provide an exhibition and study centre. The nearby church is well worth a visit. There has been a church at Daresbury since 1159, but the present building dates from 1872, with the exception of the tower, which was constructed during the 16th century. The church contains the famous 'Lewis Carroll Window', which was constructed in 1934, and shows scenes from *Alice's Adventures in Wonderland*. Various booklets and postcards are on sale, and a glance through the visitors' book shows that people have come to this place from the far corners of the globe. The church contains rich woodwork, and there is a ring of eight bells, four of which date from 1725. During more recent times, Daresbury has become well known for its nuclear research laboratory, which looks at peaceful methods of harnessing this potent source of energy.

Originally a farmhouse, the Ring O'Bells inn serves lunchtime and evening food from Monday to Saturday, and on Sunday between 12 noon and 9 pm. The inn was well known to travellers on the old road to Chester – which passed in front of the premises – before traffic was diverted along the A56 bypass. The choice of food is wide and varied and there are 'special' dishes to tempt the palate. Being a Greenalls house there is also a wide range of drinks from which to choose. The inn is tastefully furnished and there is a most attractive garden which can be utilised during warm weather. Telephone: 01925 740256.

- HOW TO GET THERE: Daresbury village centre lies to the east of the A56 between Warrington and Frodsham, 4 miles from Warrington and one mile from junction 11 of the M56 motorway.
- PARKING: There is a car park at the Ring O'Bells inn (for patrons). Alternatively, there is a large car park between the inn and the church.
- LENGTH OF THE WALK: 6½ miles. Map: OS Landranger 108 Liverpool (GR 580828).

THE WALK

1. From the Ring O'Bells inn, turn right to walk along the main street of the village. Pass a mixture of cottages and other dwellings and continue past the school. On passing the last dwelling in the village, enter a field on the left through a kissing-gate at the side of a field gate. Two paths commence at this point. Bear right now in the direction of Newton Lane and cross a large field to go through a kissing-gate which is set in a crossing hedgerow. Keep across the next field to a gate which can be seen in a crossing fence about 150 yards away. On passing through the gate keep close to a fence, and trees, on the left. Pass close to a pond and arrive at a crossing lane through a kissing-gate. Walk

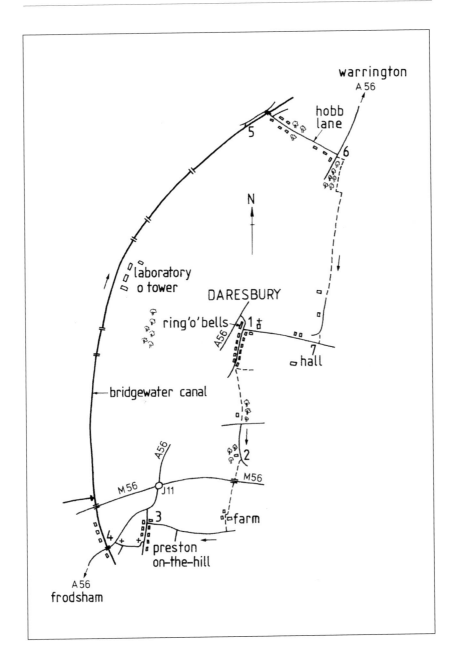

The attractive garden at the Ring O'Bells pub.

straight over the lane to enter Newton Lane and keep on past a gate on the right which is private.

2. A little further on, leave the lane to the right, through a gate, to follow a track which takes you under the M56 motorway. Go through a facing gate now, to continue along a grassy track, where a farm can be seen ahead. Pass through another gate and follow a straight length of track which leads towards the farm. Go through a gate in front of the farm and bear right, to pass between outbuildings. Pass through two more gates and join a lane which takes you away from the farm. Arrive at a crossing lane, where the way is right. Keep on past New Manor Road and arrive at a T-junction in the village of Preston-on-the-Hill.

3. Turn left in the direction of Dutton and Northwich. The village is a mix of the old and the new and contains some interesting cottages. A few yards after passing the head of a lane on the right which descends towards Chester, turn right through a gap in a low wall and descend onto its laneside pavement. Immediately on passing a road which goes off to the left called Waterfront, arrive at a T-junction. Turn left here, to cross a bridge which takes you over the Trent and Mersey Canal.

4. Descend onto the canal towpath, by Canalside Cottages, and turn left to walk under the bridge. The towpath merges with a canalside lane which takes you under the motorway, after which there is a junction of canals. This is the point at which the Trent and Mersey Canal joins the Bridgewater Canal. Walk over a footbridge here, to continue along the towpath in the same general direction as before.

You are now walking alongside an extension of the famous canal which was engineered by James Brindley to distribute coal from the Duke of Bridgewater's estates at Worsley, near Manchester. The canal used to enter the river Mersey through a series of locks at Runcorn; alas, these locks have since been abandoned.

Follow the canal for almost 3 miles, passing under George Gleaves' Bridge, Keckwick Hill Bridge, Keckwick Bridge, a road bridge and Moorefield Bridge. Also, along this section of the route, you will pass close to the nuclear research laboratory with its tall, futuristic tower and well-maintained gardens.

5. About 80 yards before arriving at the next bridge, leave the towpath to the left, through a gap in a fence, and turn right to follow a roadside pavement. Turn right now, to cross Moore Bridge and enter Hobb Lane. Pass Canalside, and gently climb along Hobb Lane. Arrive at a crossing road. Cross the road, taking care, and go through a gate at the side of a field gate.

6. Walk up a facing track. After 200 yards the track reaches level ground. There are trees on the right here. Turn right on passing the trees and walk along a field edge with the trees on your immediate right. After 350 yards the trees finish. Go through a kissing-gate and turn left to walk along a field edge, keeping a hedge on the left. Turn right at the field corner and continue with a hedge on the left. The path leads to a facing field gate. Go through a kissing-gate here and enter a gravel track which passes between hedgerows. Shortly pass stables, which are topped by an attractive ornate clock, and continue past a farm. A facing macadam drive takes you past a dwelling and begins to turn to the right. Keep forward here, along a narrow path which leads to a crossing road.

7. Turn right and follow the roadside pavement. Over to the left can be seen the magnificent Georgian building of Daresbury Hall, which was built in 1760.

A short descent along the roadside pavement takes you back to the starting point in Daresbury village.

PLACES OF INTEREST

About 3 miles from Daresbury, and signed from junction 11 of the M56 motorway, are the excavated remains of *Norton Priory*. The site was an important Augustinian foundation from 1134 to its dissolution in 1536. There is paid access to a museum, priory remains, woodland gardens, contemporary art, a picnic area, family events, a croquet area and a walled garden. The site is open every day from 12 noon to 5 pm on weekdays between April and October, and 6 pm at weekends and on public holidays. Between November and March the site is open from 12 noon to 4 pm daily, but closed from 24 to 26 December and on 1 January. Telephone: 01928 569895.

ADLINGTON AND THE MACCLESFIELD CANAL

The first section of the walk takes you across lush green fields along a path which leads to the tiny hamlet of Whiteley Green. A 2 mile stroll along the towpath of the Macclesfield Canal then provides a fine platform for magnificent views across to the hills of the Peak District. The return leg is along a section of the Middlewood Way, a former railway line, before returning to Adlington over field paths and tracks.

The Macclesfield Canal

Situated where the foothills of the Peak District meet the Cheshire Plain, the countryside around Adlington is truly idyllic. The village consists of a number of tiny hamlets scattered over 4,000 acres of undulating farmland. In days gone by, coal mining was carried out in the area and this was controlled by the Legh family of Adlington Hall. The Hall, which is situated along a minor road towards Wilmslow

35

about ½ mile from the Legh Arms, has been the home of the Legh family since 1315 and contains a fine organ which is known to have been played by George Frederick Handel when he visited Adlington in the mid 18th century. Just over one mile from the Legh Arms there are two historic transport routes which run approximately parallel to each other between Macclesfield and Marple: one is the Macclesfield Canal, the other the course of an old railway line which has been developed into a scenic country trail open to walkers, cyclists and horse riders.

Three fine hostelries – the Legh Arms (telephone: 01625 829211), the Windmill Inn (telephone: 01625 574222) and the Miner's Arms (telephone: 01625 872731) – are all situated on this circular route. All three establishments serve food throughout the day and offer a wide variety of choice. Each inn also has a garden area and children are well catered for. It's a difficult choice, but remember, all three can be visited during the course of the walk!

- HOW TO GET THERE: The village of Adlington straddles the A523 midway between Macclesfield and Hazel Grove.
- PARKING: There is a roadside parking loop which is on the Hazel Grove side of the Legh Arms Hotel at the side of the A523.
- LENGTH OF THE WALK: 6½ miles. Maps: OS Landranger 109 Manchester and 118 Stoke-on-Trent (GR 912806).

THE WALK

1. On leaving the car, walk past the front of the Legh Arms Hotel and then turn left, to enter Brookledge Lane. Pass over the railway and keep forward past Legh Road. Turn next right along Wych Lane. Follow the lane past detached dwellings to arrive at Broughton Road, which is on the right. Keep forward here and enter a facing gravel track. The track becomes a lane and very gradually climbs past a secluded dwelling on the left called Wych Cottage. The lane has become a track again which shortly turns sharply to the right. There is a facing stile here, but ignore this and follow the track as it turns to the right. After only a further 80 yards arrive at a stile on the left.

2. Cross the stile and climb up a grass bank to enter a rough field. The path generally follows the left hand side of the field and leads to a stile at the field corner. Go over the stile and continue, in the same general direction as before, to follow the left hand edge of the next field. After 200 yards go over a stile and plank-bridge on the left to follow the right

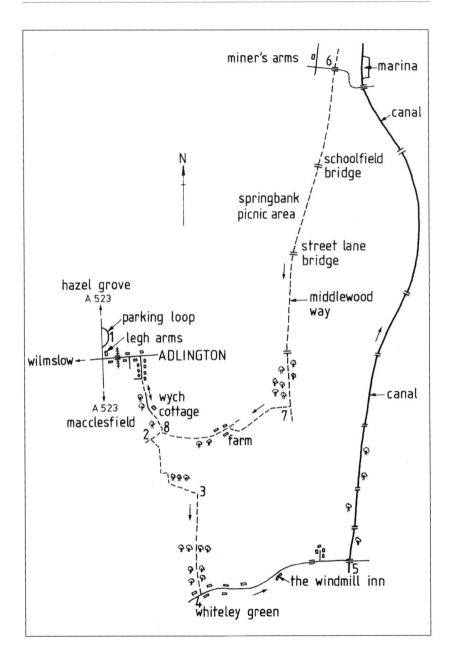

One of the five stone bridges on the Macclesfield Canal engineered by William Crosley.

hand side of a field for 150 yards. Turn right now and cross a stile. Walk along the left hand edge of the next field where an electricity pylon can be seen ahead about 250 yards away. Where a hedge and trees on the left turn away to the left, bear left and cross a field to arrive at a facing field gate and stile which is 50 yards to the left of the field corner.

3. Turn right in front of the gate and stile and then go over a stile in a crossing fence. Keeping a hedgerow on your immediate left follow a field edge. On approaching the field corner bear right to go over a plank-bridge and stile. Continue along the edge of the next field, again, keeping a hedgerow on your left. Pass over a stile which is about 20 yards to the right of the field corner and cross a rough field in the same general direction as before heading towards trees. Go over a stile and plank-bridge at the edge of the trees and then climb up steps to enter a field. Keep on, across the next field, and go over a stile to enter a wood. Follow a well-defined path through the wood and then emerge from the trees along a narrow path at the side of a dwelling. Arrive at a crossing lane in the tiny hamlet of Whiteley Green.

4. Turn left along the lane and pass Swingate Cottage. Continue and,

after ¼ mile, arrive at the Windmill inn. About 200 yards after passing the inn, follow the lane over a stone bridge. There is a small development of houses on the left now. A little further on, arrive at a bridge which carries the lane over the Macclesfield Canal. Do not cross the bridge but leave the lane to the right and descend onto the canal towpath.

5. Turn left and pass under the bridge – which is number 25.

The Macclesfield Canal was completed in 1831 under the superintendence of Thomas Telford. The canal joins the Peak Forest Canal at Marple and runs southwards through Bollington and Macclesfield to join a branch of the Trent and Mersey Canal near Kidsgrove. Canal enthusiasts travel great distances to study the canal's graceful stone bridges, many of which were designed by the engineer William Crosley. The views from the canal, especially across to the hills of the Peak District, are superb.

Follow the canal towpath for 2 miles and pass under bridges 24, 23, 22, 21, 20 and 19 to arrive at bridge 18. Do not pass under bridge 18 but climb up steps to its left to arrive at a crossing lane. Turn left away from the bridge and follow the lane as it turns to the left across a bridge. The way is to the right now, to descend onto the Middlewood Way. However, if refreshment is required walk a few yards further on to turn next right into Wood Lane North where the Miner's Arms inn is situated.

6. To continue, descend onto the Middlewood Way and turn right to walk under the bridge you have walked across.

The Middlewood Way is a former railway line which was converted into an attractive linear park. The way provides a 10 mile traffic-free route between Marple and Macclesfield.

The next 2 miles of the walk follow the course of the Middlewood Way and take you under Schoolfield Bridge, past Springbank Picnic Area and under Street Lane Bridge. About 350 yards after passing under the next bridge (No 9) – which has had a central brick supporting wall added to it during recent years – leave the Middlewood Way to the right, where a sign points to Harrop Green.

7. Go over a stile at the side of a field gate and gradually descend across a large, undulating field. Pass to the left of a crossing fence which juts out into the field. Bear slightly left now, and continue, to

arrive at a stile which is set close to tall trees. Cross the stile and bear left across a field to where, after 100 yards, there is a hedgerow. Turn right and follow the edge of the field, keeping the hedgerow on your left. Farm buildings can be seen now, ahead to the left.

Pass under power cables and go over a stile to arrive at a crossing track. Turn left along the track. There is a farmhouse on the left here, but keep forward to go over a stile at the side of a facing gate. Follow a track past a large barn which is on the right and after 100 yards go over a stile at the side of a field gate. Walk forward, keeping trees and then hedges and a gate on your left, to arrive, after 250 yards, at the field corner. Go over a stile on the right here, to arrive at a bend in a crossing track.

8. You have now joined a track which you walked along earlier. Keep forward to shortly pass Wych Cottage and then retrace your steps, via Wych Lane and Brookledge Lane, back to where the car is parked.

PLACES OF INTEREST

About 7 miles by road from Adlington, and accessible via the A523 to Hazel Grove and then the A6 towards Disley, is *Lyme Park*. There is an imposing Hall set within almost 1,400 acres of deer park, moorland and lovely formal gardens. The Hall is the largest house in Cheshire and the south front, with its mixture of columns and large pediment, is reflected by the waters of a large lake in front of it. The Hall contains four centuries of period interiors – Mortlake tapestries, Grinling Gibbons carvings and a unique collection of English clocks. The estate is open every day of the year from 8 am to dusk but the entrance time for the Hall and gardens vary. Telephone: 01663 766492.

THE RIVER WEAVER AT FRODSHAM BRIDGE

From Frodsham Bridge, the walk takes you beside the river Weaver before turning inland across field paths to join a cross-country lane which gradually climbs to the hamlet of Bradley. A gentle descent back to the bridge is along paths and tracks – from where there are long views across the Weaver valley.

Frodsham Bridge

Although only a small town, Frodsham boasts one of the widest roads in England – Main Street, the origins of which go back to the 11th century. On either side of Main Street there are some 17th-century timber-framed cottages and an assortment of Georgian houses, whilst at one end of the street stands a large boulder – thought to have been deposited by glacial action about 12,000 years ago. Frodsham has 14 pubs, the oldest being the Queen's Head, which was built at the beginning of the 17th century.

The early development of the town was inextricably linked with the river Weaver. During medieval times, when Frodsham was a thriving port, salt and cheese were exported via the river. The Romans were aware of its strategic location, as were the Normans – who built a castle which looked out across the valley of the Weaver and beyond to the estuary of the river Mersey.

A stroll around the town would make an interesting prelude prior to driving to the parking place and setting off on the walk. A good choice for refreshment is the Bear's Paw, on Main Street, which dates from 1632. The name derives from the crest of Earl Rivers of the Savage family, who were lords of the manor of Frodsham. There are old stables in the courtyard at the rear of the inn and a snug bar overlooks a garden and patio. There are elaborate carved wooden fireplaces and other artefacts which add to its charm. A wide range of meals are served daily at lunchtime. Telephone: 01928 731404.

- HOW TO GET THERE: There is good access to Frodsham. The A56, on its way between Warrington and Chester, runs through it – whilst the M56, which runs along its northern outskirts, also gives access (via junction 12). The motorway access road converges with the A56 at a swing bridge which carries the A56 over the Weaver Canal. Less than ½ mile further south is Frodsham Bridge – which carries the A56 over the river Weaver.
- PARKING: Roadside parking is available on Mill Lane, a loop road which leaves the A56 close to the bridge and runs past the Aston Arms Hotel and Frodsham Garden Centre prior to rejoining the A56.
- LENGTH OF THE WALK: 4¼ miles. Map: OS Landranger 117 Chester (GR 530786).

THE WALK

1. On leaving the car, walk past the Aston Arms Hotel and arrive at the main road. Cross the road, taking care, and turn right to pass over Frodsham Bridge – which carries the main road over the river Weaver. Immediately on crossing the bridge, turn left, and pass over a concreted area then through a metal gate. Walk across a gravel-strewn area and pass through a metal gate to join a well-defined path between hawthorn trees. The path runs parallel with the river, which is about 20 yards away, over to the left. Go over a footbridge and then pass through a metal kissing-gate. Emerge from the trees and pass over a

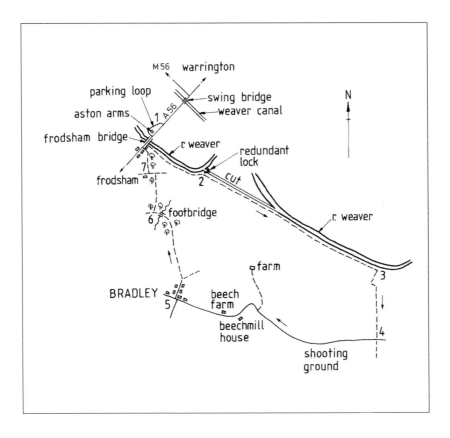

stile. The path is now closer to the water's edge. Go through a kissing-gate to arrive at a redundant lock.

2. Keep to the right of the lock and then pass through a gateway to continue alongside the lock.

This lock, and the 'cut' leading from it, was constructed to make the river navigable for sea-going vessels. The lock was made redundant when the other approaches of the estuary were canalised – with the resulting navigation joining the main course of the river upstream from the lock.

There is a stile now, and a path on the right which goes to Bradley, but keep forward over another stile, to follow the cut which leads from the lock. Keep on, past the tiny brick building of Bradley Orchard Pumping Station. The cut which leads from the lock joins the main course of the river shortly. An obvious riverside path leads over a stile

Footpath sign near Bradley.

and then takes you through an avenue of hawthorn trees. A little further on, and about ¾ mile after passing the redundant lock, the river begins to gently bend to the left. At this point you arrive at a facing stile and gate.

3. Do not cross this stile but turn right, away from the riverside, to follow the edge of a field. After 100 yards go over a stile on the left which is immediately followed by a footbridge. Turn right now and follow a well-defined track. Pass through a metal kissing-gate at the side of a field gate. Follow the edge of a large field, keeping a hedgerow on your immediate right. A stile at the field corner gives access to a hedged-in lane.

4. There is a facing metal kissing-gate here, but turn right to follow the lane. The lane takes you past Catton Hall Shooting Ground – which is over to the left. Go over a cattle-grid and then follow the lane as it climbs. There is a track on the right shortly, which descends to a farm, but ignore this and continue to climb along the lane. Pass Beechmill House and then Beech Farm, after which the lane is along more level terrain, from where there are views over to Beacon Hill on the left. The lane takes you into the tiny hamlet of Bradley. Immediately on passing

a wall-mounted post-box there is a junction of ways – where Watery Lane goes off to the left.

5. Turn sharp right here, to follow a lane between dwellings. On passing Dingle Farm and Dingle Barn, there is a junction of footpaths. Take the left hand path and descend between hedges. The path becomes hemmed-in by high bankings and trees then takes you over a footbridge, after which it gradually climbs. About 90 yards after crossing the footbridge leave the path to the right, up steps, where there is also a footpath sign.

6. Follow the edge of a large field now, keeping a fence on your immediate right. Pass through a gap in a crossing hedgerow and follow a well-defined path which gradually descends in the direction of a railway viaduct which can be seen straight ahead. After 150 yards, there is a hedgerow on your immediate right. Pass through a gap at the field corner and continue in the same direction as before to descend along the next field edge where there is a row of trees on your immediate right. At the field corner, bear right to follow a path through trees. Arrive at a track and turn left. Houses come into view.

Some of the memorabilia on display at the Mouldsworth Motor Museum.

7. About 80 yards before the houses are reached leave the track to the right, through a kissing-gate, and follow a well-defined path which descends through undergrowth, bushes and trees. The path becomes hemmed-in by trees and is then raised above the surrounding marshy area on wooden planks, after which there is a metal kissing-gate to pass through which is close to dwellings. A narrow passageway between the dwellings leads to a crossing road. On the right is Frodsham Bridge – which you crossed earlier in the walk. A short stroll takes you back to the car.

PLACES OF INTEREST

The *Mouldsworth Motor Museum* is about 5½ miles (by road) to the south of Frodsham. It is reached via the B5393 and is situated on a minor road which connects Ashton with Mouldsworth. It is a mecca for anyone with an interest in the history of transport. There are examples of early motor cars, Dinky toys, old tools, magazines and signs from a bygone age together with a reconstruction of a 1920s garage which really captures the ambience of an era long since gone. Telephone: 01928 731781.

LITTLE LEIGH AND THE WEAVER VALLEY: BY RIVER AND CANAL

Commencing close by the river Weaver, the first 2 miles of the walk are along a scenic path which follows the course of the river to Saltersford Locks. A second waterway, the Trent and Mersey Canal, is then visited where a towpath stroll is intermixed with a cross-country path which climbs to Little Leigh before descending back to the parking place.

The Leigh Arms by the river Weaver.

Situated 3 miles to the north-west of Northwich, the tiny village of Little Leigh is tucked away on elevated ground on the northern side of the Weaver valley. Its dwellings are a mixture of the old and the new, and its church is of simple red-brick construction. There is a village hall, which was once a school, built by voluntary contributions in 1840 with the land being donated by the lord of the manor.

The pace of life in the village is relaxed and easy going being more in tune with the speed of the vessels plying along the adjacent waterways of the Trent and Mersey Canal and river Weaver than the traffic rushing along the nearby A49 trunk road.

The Leigh Arms, which can boast a long history, has been extended and developed over recent years. Hand-pulled real ale can be purchased and the inn provides a wide range of meals seven days a week – including a traditional Sunday lunch. Outside, there is an attractive beer garden which is situated by the river (telephone: 01606 853327). A few short strides from the Leigh Arms, and situated on the other side of Willowgreen Lane, is the appealing Horns Inn – which offers an alternative refreshment venue. Telephone: 01606 852192.

- HOW TO GET THERE: Approaching from Warrington, the A49 passes over the M6 (junction 10) and continues past Weaverham to Sandiway and its intersection with the A556. Between the motorway and Sandiway, the A49 is carried over the river Weaver by a large swing bridge. Close by is Willowgreen Lane and the Leigh Arms inn.
- PARKING: The Leigh Arms has a large car park (for patrons). Alternatively, there is limited parking available at the head of Willowgreen Lane.
- LENGTH OF THE WALK: 5 miles. Map: OS Landranger 118 Stoke-on-Trent (GR 601761).

THE WALK

1. On leaving the car, enter Willowgreen Lane and at its junction with the A49 go through a gate on the left to descend onto the towpath of the river Weaver. Turn left and walk away from the swing bridge to follow a riverside path. The path stays close by the riverside and there are a number of gates and stiles to negotiate. After almost 2 miles arrive at a large footbridge which crosses an inlet to the main river.

2. Cross the footbridge and continue along the riverside to shortly arrive at Saltersford Locks. There are a number of dwellings here and a picnic site. Follow a macadam lane over a substantial bridge and then follow it along the riverside. Shortly, the lane turns to the left and climbs away from the riverside. Follow the lane as it climbs and arrive on the towpath of the Trent and Mersey Canal.

3. Turn left and keep along the towpath. The canal is quite wide at this point which allows vessels to turn if required. Shortly, the canal enters

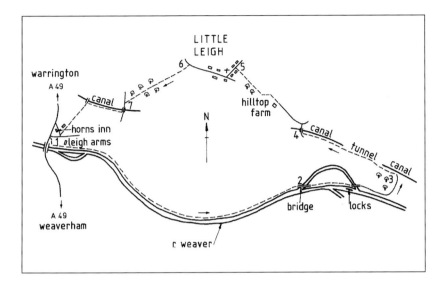

Saltersford Tunnel which is 424 yards long. The path climbs to the left of the tunnel and then climbs forwards between trees and hedges. Pass through a kissing-gate and continue along a hedged-in path. The route follows the same course as the tunnel – which is below your feet! On the right shortly, there is a tapered brick structure which is a ventilation shaft from the tunnel. The path descends and rejoins the canal towpath close by the outlet of the tunnel. Follow the towpath to the next bridge (number 204).

4. Leave the towpath here and walk over the bridge. Immediately on crossing the bridge there is a junction of ways. Turn left here to climb along a rough lane. Keep forward to walk by Hilltop Farm to enter a facing grassy path. Go over a stile at the left hand side of a gate and follow a hedged-in path. The path turns to the right. Pass over a stile at the side of a gate and follow a fenced-in path along a field edge. The path becomes a hedged-in track and leads to a lane on the outskirts of the village of Little Leigh.

5. Turn left and follow the lane into the village. On the right shortly is the simple red-brick building of St Michael and All Angels church. A few strides further on there is a junction in front of the village hall, where the way is right. A tablet on the wall tells us that the hall was once Little Leigh School – erected by voluntary contributions in 1840

The Trent and Mersey Canal

with land and timber given by Lord Leigh. Pass the post-box and follow the lane out of the village. About 100 yards further on, where the lane gently turns to the right, there is a track on the left which is headed by a footpath sign.

6. Enter the track – which is hedged in. The track is a fine platform for views across the Weaver valley. Across to the left, in the middle-distance, can be seen the tower of Weaverham church whilst straight ahead, on the skyline, is the whale-like form of the Overton Hills. The track finishes at a field gate but keep forward here to follow a facing path which is fenced in. The path descends through trees and emerges at a crossing lane.

7. Turn left and immediately cross a bridge which takes you over the canal. On crossing the bridge go through a gap on the right at the side of a gate to rejoin the towpath of The Trent and Mersey Canal. Walk away from the bridge (number 207) and walk under the next bridge (number 208). Leave the towpath here to join a path which takes you away from the bridge. The path is quite densely hedged-in here where the trees meet above your head. Emerge from the trees to follow a path which keeps along a field edge. The path takes you to the left of a

garden shortly where the path is hedged-in. Emerge from the path and walk forward to arrive back at Willowgreen Lane and the car.

PLACES OF INTEREST

Some 5 miles to the east of the parking place and accessible via the A533 towards Northwich, is the village of Anderton. Close by the village is one of the masterpieces of canal design, the *Anderton Lift*. The lift, which was completed during 1875, was constructed to transfer barges between the canal and the river Weaver, and work is being undertaken with a view to restoring it to its former glory.

The Anderton Lift

WALK 8

ACTON BRIDGE AND THE RIVER WEAVER

This pleasant ramble through the mid-Cheshire countryside takes in an attractive stretch of the Dutton Bridleway – which follows the northern bank of the river Weaver to Dutton Locks. The route then switches to the southern bank of the river before gently climbing via lanes, paths and tracks back to the village of Acton Bridge.

The river Weaver and Dutton railway viaduct.

The village of Acton Bridge sits atop high ground overlooking the scenic valley of the river Weaver. Its delightfully named roads such as Pear Tree Lane, Orchard Avenue and Strawberry Lane run past well-kept gardens which are a pleasure to view.

Many old industries used to flourish in Acton Bridge. There was a zinc factory, a sawmill, a saltpetre works, a flour mill and a bakehouse – which delivered fresh bread by horse and cart. Although these once thriving industries have long since gone the blacksmith's forge is still well patronised.

Acton Bridge is at the hub of a predominantly farming community and its villagers have worked hard during recent years. The village hall has been enlarged and refurbished and the Methodist chapel restored, resulting in a most agreeable village ambience.

The Maypole Inn is over 250 years old and was, up to 1827, known as The Cheese. Owned by Greenalls, the inn has a most attractive interior, the walls being lined with old china, brass and copperware. There are low-beamed ceilings and antique furniture, and real fires add to the atmosphere on cold days. Outside, there is a secluded patio garden at the rear where the floral displays can be admired. Food is cooked to order and is served daily at lunchtime and during the evening. A wide choice is on offer and there is a specials board where the menu is changed daily. A keenly priced menu is on offer to senior citizens every lunchtime from Monday to Saturday. Telephone: 01606 853114.

- HOW TO GET THERE: Approaching from Warrington, the A49 passes over the M6 (junction 10) and continues past Weaverham to Sandiway and its intersection with the A556. Between the motorway and Sandiway the A49 is carried over the river Weaver by a large swing bridge. Close to the Bridge, on the Weaverham side, Acton Lane climbs towards the village of Acton Bridge. Enter Acton Lane, pass Strawberry Lane, and turn next left along Hill Top Road to arrive at the Maypole Inn.
- PARKING: The Maypole Inn has a large car park (for patrons).
  Alternatively, there is limited parking available at the head of Willowgreen Lane between the Leigh Arms and Horns Inn, close by the swing bridge over the river Weaver. You would then start the walk at point 3.
- LENGTH OF THE WALK: 6 miles. Maps: OS Landranger 117 Chester and 118 Stoke-on-Trent (GR 598749).

THE WALK

1. On leaving the inn, turn left to follow the pavement alongside Hill Top Road. Keep on past the parish room and Old Lane and at the next junction keep forward to enter Cliff Road. Continue, to where, shortly after passing a road on the right called Bancroft, there is a stile on the right which is situated between a house (number 44) and a bungalow (number 42).

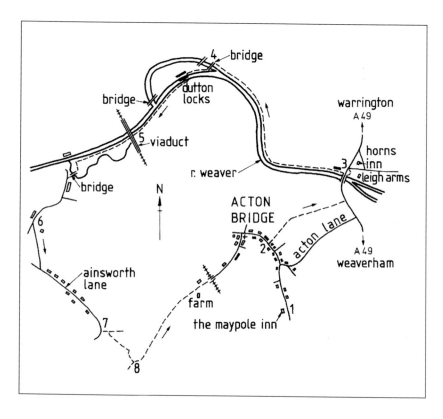

2. Go over the stile and descend, keeping a garden fence on your immediate left. On crossing the next stile, the swing bridge which carries the A49 over the river Weaver comes into view. Keep close to a hedgerow and cross another stile and then descend along a facing gully and at the bottom of the descent go over a stile in a crossing fence. The path takes you to a broad, flat wooden bridge and then leads across level, marshy terrain. Go over a plank-bridge and stile to continue along a fenced-in path. Climb steps which lead to a crossing road via a stile. Cross the road, taking care, and turn left to follow the roadside pavement. Go over the swing bridge to arrive at a gate on the right just before Willowgreen Lane is reached.

3. Go through the gate and descend onto the towpath of the river Weaver. Turn right and walk under the swing bridge to follow the Dutton Bridleway – a narrow macadam lane which stays close by the river. After one mile arrive at a bridge which spans a loop of the river.

Budworth Mere

4. Cross the bridge and arrive at Dutton Locks. Cross over to the other side of the river now, via the walkways on top of the lock gates. Turn right, pass through a gate in a fence, and follow a riverside path away from the locks. Straight ahead is a large stone viaduct which carries the Warrington to Crewe railway line across the Weaver valley. Over to the right there is a large, twin-arched footbridge where the previously mentioned loop of the river rejoins the main navigation. Go through a gate in front of the viaduct.

5. Pass under the viaduct. On the left now there is a land-locked section of the river's original course which was superseded when the river was straightened out in order to make it navigable for larger vessels. Pass through a couple of gates and then turn left to follow a path which takes you away from the riverside. On crossing a bridge turn left to follow a lane past dwellings. Keep on, past Cliff Lane which goes off to the left and follow the facing lane as it bends and gently climbs. At the top of the climb pass dwellings and arrive at a junction of lanes.

6. Fork left to where, after 250 yards, you fork left again along

Ainsworth Lane. The lane takes you past various dwellings including Damson Cottage and Pear Tree Farm. About 150 yards after passing a pair of semi-detached dwellings called Field View and Morningside, the lane begins to bend to the right. There is a track which goes off to the left here where there is a footpath sign.

7. Enter the track. After only 50 yards turn right and pass through a wooden kissing-gate and then through a second kissing-gate. With the gate at your back, walk forward across the facing field. After 150 yards pass to the left of an isolated tree. Descend, and then go over a footbridge which takes you over a stream. Follow a winding path along the edge of the next field and then go through a gate in a crossing hedgerow to arrive at a junction of paths.

8. Turn left and pass over a stone footbridge to follow a path which climbs between hedges. The path reaches level terrain and becomes a track and then a lane which shortly takes you past a farm. Cross a bridge over the railway and follow the facing lane. Pass Rookery Cottages and follow the lane into the village of Acton Bridge, passing Orchard Avenue en route. Turn right immediately on passing Acton Bridge Methodist church and keep on past Wetton Lane – which goes off to the left. Follow the roadside pavement and continue past the stile you crossed earlier in the walk and the road called Bancroft. At the next junction enter Hill Top Road which leads back to the Maypole Inn and the car.

PLACES OF INTEREST

About 6 miles from the parking place and accessible via the A533, which intersects the A49 one mile to the north of the river Weaver, and a minor road through Anderton towards Comberbach, is *Marbury Country Park*. Within the park, which covers an area of 200 acres, there are picnic sites and information boards which relate to various points of interest. The park borders Budworth Mere, where a slotted partition has been erected allowing visitors to observe the wildlife at close quarters.

WALK 9
THE WEAVER VALLEY AT KINGSLEY

From Kingsley and its old buildings, the walk descends into the valley of the river Weaver to follow a very scenic riverside path – after which lanes and field paths lead back to the village.

The Weaver valley

Kingsley is an ancient place and its history can be traced back to Saxon times. Kingsley Mill, on the outskirts of the village, is still operating and so carries on a tradition started before the time of the Norman Conquest. During the Civil War (1642–49) the villagers were staunch supporters of the Parliamentarian cause. The nucleus of the village is a mixture of old cottages and Georgian houses, whilst more modern dwellings have been constructed during recent times. You will find a church, two schools, a village store and two hostelries: the Horseshoe and the Red Bull.

The Red Bull Inn in the centre is a good choice for a tempting range of home-made meals and traditional cask ales. Lunches are served every day except Monday and Tuesday, and there is a traditional roast every Sunday. Meals can be purchased every evening except Wednesday. The inn has been refurbished during recent years and the front room contains many interesting pictures which relate the history of Kingsley – these being provided by the villagers. Outside, there is a most attractive garden which runs down to a stream, and a French boules pitch. Telephone: 01928 788097.

- HOW TO GET THERE: The village of Kingsley is just over 3 miles south-east of Frodsham (see Walk 6) – from where it is reached via the B5152 and B5153 roads.
- PARKING: There is a small public car park adjacent to the community centre. To reach it, enter Westbrook Road, which leaves the B5153 between the church and the Horseshoe Inn, and turn next left along Smithy Lane. Alternatively, if you are using the facilities of the Red Bull Inn, you may park there. The Red Bull is reached by entering a road called The Cross, which intersects with the B5153 near the post office, where a signpost points to Delamere.
- LENGTH OF THE WALK: 5 miles. Map: OS Landranger 117 Chester (GR 550748).

THE WALK

1. From the car park, enter an adjacent macadam path and turn left. After only 60 yards or so, emerge onto the B5153 between a school and a garage, not far from the Horseshoe Inn. Cross the road, taking care, and turn right to follow the roadside pavement. Keep on past The Cross, a road on the right which goes to Delamere. (This is the point at which you join the route if you have parked at the Red Bull.) Pass the Georgian building of Kingsley Hall and Town Well – a narrow lane which goes off to the right. Keep on, past a row of dwellings on the left which were built in 1790. Pass Chapel Lane and a large roadside dwelling called Brook House Farm. About 200 yards further on arrive at Ball Lane.

2. Turn left to enter Ball Lane and follow it past Tan House Farm (1751). About ¼ mile after joining the lane, leave it to the left, through a gate, to walk along a track towards Hall o'th Hay Farm. Arrive at a junction close by a dwelling on the left. The track to the right goes to the farm but walk forward here, keeping to the right of the garden hedgerow which surrounds the dwelling on the left, to pass through a gateway. Keep to the left of a barn, and then bear right through a gateway to follow a

58

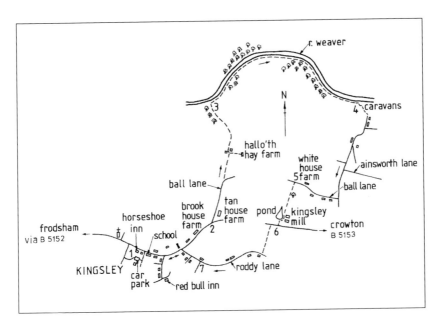

hedged-in track. Pass through another gate and gradually descend into the lovely wooded valley of the river Weaver, glimpses of which can be seen over to the left winding its way towards Frodsham. On passing over a stile at the side of a gate near the bottom of the descent, there are trees on the left. Shortly, the river comes into view.

3. Arrive close by the waterside and turn right to follow a riverside path. After 250 yards go through a metal kissing-gate to follow a path which meanders through trees but which is never far from the riverside. The opposite bank in this area is steep and densely wooded. On passing over a plank-bridge and kissing-gate leave the trees behind to follow a riverside path through more open countryside. Gradually converge with trees. Go through a kissing-gate to follow a path which runs through the trees close by the waterside. Where the trees finish pass through another kissing-gate. Keep along the edge of a field now, to where, after 200 yards, there is a kissing-gate to negotiate, which is set in a crossing hedgerow. Dwellings come into view on both sides of the river shortly, and, a little further on, the arches of Dutton railway viaduct can be seen. The path turns to the right, away from the riverside now, to where, on the left, there is a kissing-gate. There is a caravan site here, on the other side of the kissing-gate.

One of Kingsley's two pubs.

4. Go through the kissing-gate and turn right between caravans to go through a wooden gate. Follow a facing track between caravans, then pass through a gap at the side of a gate to join a lane, where the way is right. Pass dwellings, then keep on past Cliff Lane which goes off to the left and follow the facing lane as it bends and gently climbs. At the top of the climb pass dwellings and arrive at a junction of lanes. Take the right fork, to keep forward along the facing lane. Keep on, past a narrow lane which goes off to the right, and continue past Ainsworth Lane – which goes off to the left. After a further ¼ mile turn right, to enter Ball Lane. Pass the splendid building of Higher Heyes Farm and keep on past other dwellings to shortly pass White House Farm, which is on the right. About 140 yards further on, leave the lane to the left, over a stile at the side of a double gate, to enter a large field.

5. With the stile at your back, walk straight across the facing field, passing close to an isolated tree. Arrive at the field corner, where there are hedgerows, and go over two stiles in quick succession. Follow a grassy path between bushes and converge with a large pond. Walk along a raised footpath now, where the pond is on the immediate right. Pass through a gate and continue. At the head of the pond descend a flight of steps and then arrive at a crossing road. A sign here,

tells you that the large building you have just walked past is Kingsley Mill, whose origins go back hundreds of years.

6. Cross the road, taking care, and turn right to follow the roadside pavement. After 80 yards, go over a stile on the left, which is reached up a couple of steps. Follow a field edge now, where there is a row of Scotch pines on the immediate right. Pass over a stile in a crossing fence and continue along the next field edge. A gate at the field corner takes you onto a lane. Turn right along the lane. Pass a couple of bungalows and other dwellings. Arrive at a junction of lanes where a sign tells you that the lane you have just walked along is called Roddy Lane.

7. Turn right now, to enter Chapel Lane. Keep on, past Chapel Avenue, to arrive at a crossing road. Cross the road, taking care, and turn left.

You are now back on part of your initial route. A short stroll takes you back to the car.

PLACES OF INTEREST

The centre of the largest surviving tract of *Delamere Forest* lies only 2 miles to the south of Kingsley. There are a number of picnic sites and a display centre – located in the now disused Delamere station at Linmere, which is 3 miles from Kingsley on the B5152.

ALONG THE WEAVER AT VALE ROYAL

From Hartford Bridge the walk follows a lane and paths which skirt the lovely Vale Royal Abbey estate. A cross-country path then leads to the outskirts of the village of Whitegate before turning to join the banks of the river Weaver from where a scenic riverside path takes you back to the bridge.

Hartford bridge over the river Weaver

The triangular tract of land between the river Weaver from Hartford Bridge to the outskirts of Winsford and the village of Whitegate is mainly an area of unspoilt parkland. This is Vale Royal Park, once the setting of one of the finest and largest Cistercian abbeys in England. The abbey was founded by Edward I in 1277 but sadly this once magnificent building has long since disappeared, being replaced by a large private house and golf course. Nevertheless, we are fortunate that public footpaths still criss-cross this attractive area of countryside.

A good choice for refreshment in the area is the Plough Inn at Beauty Bank, Foxwist Green, near Whitegate. From the Hartford Picnic

Area drive along the A556 in the direction of Chester and after 2½ miles take the next turn to the left to follow a minor road in the direction of Whitegate and Winsford. After a further 2 miles keep forward at the second junction and then turn next left to arrive at Beauty Bank. Once a small cottage, the Plough inn has been developed into a most attractive establishment during recent years. A Robinson's house, it provides a wide range of home-made lunches, served seven days a week. Telephone: 01606 889455.

- HOW TO GET THERE: The trunk route between Manchester and Chester is made up of four roads: the A56, A556, A54 and A51. Midway between the two places the A556 bypasses Northwich to the south of the town and crosses the river Weaver at Hartford Bridge.
- PARKING: There is a large car park at Hartford Picnic Area – which is situated by the A556 less than ½ mile from Hartford Bridge in the direction of Chester.
- LENGTH OF THE WALK: 6½ miles. Map: OS Landranger 118 Stoke-on-Trent (GR 640714).

THE WALK

1. From the car park, follow the roadside verge and pavement towards Hartford Bridge. On reaching the traffic lights climb up steps on the right to enter a field through a gate. Cross the field, pass through a gate, and descend along a path which turns to the left. Go through another gate and follow a path through trees to shortly arrive at a crossing lane – where the way is right. After about ¼ mile, pass under a large stone railway viaduct. Soon the lane turns to the left, but keep straight ahead here and pass to the right of a metal gate. About 100 yards before a facing metal gate is reached (at a golf course), go through a gap on the left at the side of a gate.

2. Follow a path which quickly turns to the right. On the left now is the old course of the river Weaver – which was superseded by a new channel which was cut to make an easier passage for vessels. Go over a stile in a crossing fence, which is about 20 yards from the water's edge, and follow a well-defined path through trees. The path has been reinforced with wood strips in this area and passes close to the golf course which is on the right.

A large house which is on the site of Vale Royal Abbey can be seen across the golf course over to the right.

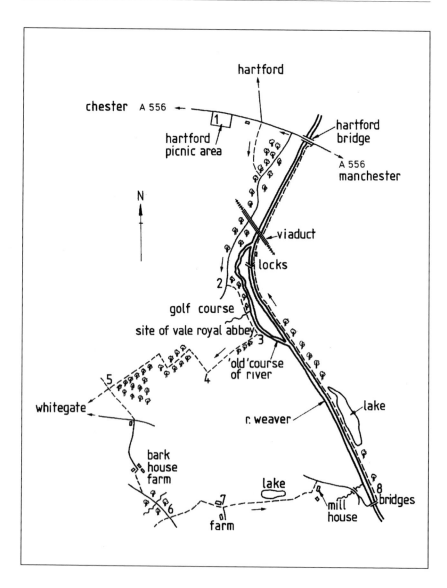

The path leads to a stream which flows along a channel prior to entering the river. Step over this channel and then climb to the right through rhododendron bushes and trees. A little further on, emerge from the trees by a stile.

3. Walk straight ahead now to follow a well-defined path which

The Plough at Beauty Bank

gradually climbs across a large field and takes you past three isolated trees. The path leads to a step-stile on the right.

4. Go over the step-stile and, bearing left, go over another step-stile to continue along a fenced-in path. There is a wood on the left now. Shortly, turn left and go over a plank-bridge to follow a path through the wood. After about 200 yards leave the wood through a gap on the right and turn left to follow a field path to arrive at a wooden electricity pole which can be seen at the corner of a wood straight ahead. Bear left now to follow a path which hugs the wood on the left.

5. Where the wood on the left finishes, turn left and leave the track to follow a path in the direction of a dwelling which can be seen across a facing field about 300 yards away near a couple of trees. Go over a stile and arrive at a crossing lane near the dwelling. Enter the facing entrance drive to Bark House Farm and continue, to arrive close by the large three-storey farmhouse. Turn right here to enter a gravel track which takes you past the front of the house.

The track turns to the left and descends to a lane. Turn left along the

A delightful stretch of the river Weaver near Hartford Bridge.

lane. After about 300 yards arrive at a point where a footpath crosses the lane.

6. Leave the lane to the left here over a stile at the side of a field gate. Keep along the edge of a large, undulating field, keeping a hedgerow and trees on your immediate left. Go over a plank-bridge and stile at the field corner and then pass through a gate in front of farm outbuildings. Follow a track alongside the outbuildings. There is a farmhouse on the right now.

7. Go over a facing stile and follow the edge of an undulating field, keeping a fence on your immediate right. On reaching the field corner go over a plank-bridge and stile then stay along the edge of the next field where a lake can be seen on the left. Cross a plank-bridge and then go over a stile in a crossing fence. Pass a telegraph pole and cross a rough field to go over another stile. Keep forward now, in the same direction as before, to follow a path between fences. Go over a stout wooden bridge, which has a gate at each end, and then turn left through a gate. Follow a track past Mill House and arrive at a crossing lane. Turn right along the lane and follow it over a bridge. Leave the lane to the left now and follow a narrow macadam lane which runs

parallel with the river Weaver. Cross two bridges to arrive at the far side of the river.

8. Turn left and follow a well-defined riverside path. Follow the riverside for almost 2 miles through a most attractive stretch of countryside. The path leads past Vale Royal Locks and then goes under a railway viaduct prior to reaching Hartford Bridge. Leave the riverside just before the bridge and climb to the right to reach the main road.

Turn left and cross the bridge and then gradually climb back to Hartford Picnic Area and the car.

PLACES OF INTEREST
One mile to the east of Hartford Bridge – in the direction of Manchester – the A556 is crossed by the A533. Turn left here in the direction of Northwich and after a further mile arrive at *Northwich Salt Museum*.

The museum relates the fascinating story of Cheshire's oldest industry. There are artefacts dating back to Roman times, models, reconstructions and audio-visual programmes. The Salt Museum is open every day except Monday: from 10 am to 5 pm on Tuesday to Friday and 2 pm to 5 pm at weekends. Telephone: 01606 41331.

REDES MERE AND OTHER LAKES

This walk presents an opportunity to stroll close to a number of lakes and a pretty stream. Firstly along the eastern shore of Redes Mere then on past the lovely lakeside setting of Capesthorne Hall after which wooded farmland is crossed to within sight of Snape Brook. The final leg of the walk is along cross-country tracks and paths which lead back to the car park on the edge of the mere.

Redes Mere

Lakes or 'meres' are numerous throughout Cheshire. Several of these are quite large, as is Redes Mere, near Siddington, which probably resulted from the processes of glaciation. This mere is extensively used by yachtsmen, fishermen and an abundance of visiting wildlife. It is also interlinked by streams with three lakes at nearby Capesthorne Hall, which in turn are connected to a feeder stream of the river Weaver called Snape Brook.

As for refreshment before or after the walk, a little over 2 miles to the south of Siddington, and straddling the A34, is the village of Marton. At its centre, and close to the oldest half-timbered church still in use in Europe, is the Davenport Arms. The inn has an attractive interior with exposed beams and cosy rooms. Bar meals can be purchased and there is also a small restaurant. Children are made welcome and there is a pleasant garden to relax in during the summer months. Telephone 01260 224269.

- HOW TO GET THERE: The A34 runs north/south and connects Alderley Edge with Congleton. Midway between these two places is the village of Siddington. Enter Fanshawe Lane, where a sign tells you that Henbury is 3 miles away.
- PARKING: There is a long, narrow parking strip opposite the waters of Redes Mere. Alternatively, there is a picnic site with parking facilities between the mere and the A34 which is open from spring until autumn.
- LENGTH OF THE WALK: 3½ miles. Map: OS Landranger 118 Stoke-on-Trent (GR 848713).

THE WALK

1. On leaving the car, turn right and follow Fanshawe Lane past the head of Redes Mere. This is a popular place – where well-fed waterfowl of many species take easy pickings from the visitors. Go over a stile on the left to follow a broad, grassy path which takes you along a field edge where there are glimpses of Redes Mere through trees on the left. On crossing the next stile the path is fenced-in on both sides. Cross another stile and keep left along a fenced-in path through trees. Pass through a gate and emerge from the trees. On the left here is the base of Redes Mere Sailing Club. Walk forward to join a track and follow it as it keeps parallel to the eastern shore of the mere. About 40 yards before reaching a gate turn left.

2. Pass over a footbridge which leads over an outlet stream from the mere and follow a path through trees. There is a fine view along the expanse of Redes Mere from this section of the path. Shortly, after passing over another footbridge, arrive at a crossing road. Cross the road, taking care, and pass over a stile which takes you into a large field. Follow the field edge, keeping a fence and trees on your immediate right. The path leads directly to the edge of a lake where there is a rather splendid view across the water to an old-fashioned wooden boat-house which is set amongst trees.

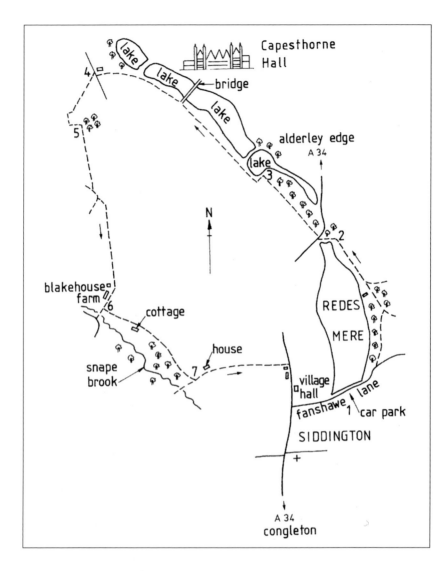

3. Turn left and follow a path which skirts around the edge of the lake and then go over the second stile on the right. The next section of the route is very scenic indeed. On the immediate right is a large lake overlooked by the magnificent Capesthorne Hall, whose towers and distinctive red-brick façade present a most appealing vista. The Hall, the home of the Bromley-Davenports, is unusual in that it was redesigned in a Jacobean style following a near disastrous fire in 1861.

Capesthorne Hall and Lake.

A waterside path takes you over a stile in a crossing fence and leads to a metal kissing-gate close to where a graceful bridge of brick and stone spans the lake. Keep on, along the lakeside, and follow an obvious path to shortly pass over a stile at the side of a pair of facing gates. A short length of track leads past a bungalow to a crossing lane.

4. Cross the lane and pass over a stile to enter a field. Bearing left, cross the field and go over a stile in a crossing fence. Continue in the same direction and then go over a stile to the right of a large tree. Pass over a stile at the side of a gate and continue, keeping a fence on your immediate left, and after only 40 yards go over a stile in a crossing hedgerow. Turn left and follow the edge of a large field keeping a hedgerow on your immediate left. After 60 yards follow the hedgerow as it turns sharply to the left. After a further 60 yards arrive at a facing stile and plank-bridge which give access to a wood. Do not cross this stile but turn to your right in front of it.

5. Walk close to a telegraph pole and then go over a stile in a crossing fence. After a further 80 yards cross a stile and then, 40 yards further on, enter a track over another stile. The track quickly turns to the right where there is a stile at the side of a gateway. There is a junction of

The Davenport Arms at Marton.

ways here. There is a facing track, which gently climbs, and a stile to its immediate left. Cross the stile to enter a large field and bear left to arrive at a stile at the side of a gate which is about 80 yards to the left of farm outbuildings. Cross the stile, walk over a track and pass over two further stiles to follow a facing track which takes you to the left of Blakehouse Farm. The track becomes a drive between grassy banks and gently descends to a junction of ways.

6. Turn left and follow the track in the direction of a thatched cottage which can be seen about 200 yards away. Follow the track past the cottage. About 120 yards further on, the track leads to a facing field gate. Keep to the right of this gate to follow a path which leads along the edge of a wood – where the ground on your right slopes down to a winding stream called Snape Brook. Arrive at a junction of paths.

7. Keep left to gently climb along a path where there are banks, trees and hedges on both sides. Shortly, on the left, there is a dwelling. Keep forward here to follow a track which leads away from the dwelling. The track takes you to a crossing road. Turn right here and follow the roadside pavement. Keep on past Siddington Village Hall and then turn next left, taking care, to enter Fanshawe Lane.

A short stroll takes you back to the car park.

PLACES OF INTEREST

Having observed its towers and distinctive façade during the course of the walk, a visit to *Capesthorne Hall*, park and gardens makes for an interesting insight into one of Cheshire's stately homes. The Hall possesses a fascinating collection of paintings, furniture and tapestries whilst the adjoining park, gardens and woodlands extend to some 60 acres. Access to the estate is from the A34 just over one mile to the north of Siddington. It is usually open from the end of March to the end of October on Sundays and Mondays and all bank holidays. The gardens are open between 12 noon and 5 pm, and the Hall between 1.30 pm and 3.30 pm. Telephone: 01625 861221.

The lake and boathouse at Capesthorne

WALK 12

CHESTER AND THE RIVER DEE

*You could choose to do just one section of this figure-of-eight route –
but to combine the two would give you a walk of exceptional variety.
The first part is a circuit of Chester's medieval walls, with numerous
opportunities to take a closer look at some of the city's interesting
'nooks and crannies' before continuing – including a chance to
explore Chester Cathedral. Add all these attractions to a ramble
through historic parkland and a picturesque riverside stroll and you
have the ingredients for a most fulfilling excursion.*

The river Dee at Chester.

Chester has a rich architectural heritage where a mixture of 17th-
century dwellings, with mainly Victorian black-and-white façades,
blend with stately Georgian houses which form a backdrop to the
imposing building of the cathedral. There are also traces of the Roman
occupation and a virtually complete circuit of city walls. During the
Middle Ages, vessels from all over Europe sailed up the river Dee to
trade at the port of Chester and a fine sandstone bridge survives from

this period. Today the waters of the Dee are mainly used by pleasure craft which can be hired from a riverside promenade.

The Boathouse, located at the start – and end – of the walk, was, as its name implies, once used to store rivercraft. Built during the 17th century, the pub overlooks the Dee, which is always a source of interest. Food is served every lunchtime and there are many dishes to tempt the tastebuds. The starters include home-made soup, home-made pâté and garlic mushrooms. Main courses consist of deep-fried cod, breast of chicken, steak and kidney pie, gammon, lasagne, chilli and a selection of Yorkshire puddings with different fillings. There is a good choice of liquid refreshment including a wide selection of bottled beers, lagers, ciders and soft drinks. There is also a comprehensive wine list. Children are very welcome and have their own menu. There is a family room, a no-smoking area and a large outside patio area close by the riverside. Food is served every day between 12 noon and 9 pm. Telephone: 01244 328709.

- HOW TO GET THERE: The A51 Nantwich to Chester road enters the city of Chester on the eastern side in an area called Boughton. From the A51 enter Dee Lane, which commences opposite a pub called City Tavern. A sign at the head of Dee Lane points to 'River Dee and The Groves'. On reaching the bottom of Dee Lane bear right to arrive close by the river and the Boathouse inn.
- PARKING: There is a large car park at the inn (for patrons). There are numerous alternative parking places, although, at peak periods, these are at a premium.
- LENGTH OF THE WALK: 5½ miles or 7½ miles if you include a circuit of the city walls. Map: OS Landranger 117 Chester (GR 412661).

THE WALK

1. From the Boathouse, follow the riverside promenade and keep on past a large suspension footbridge which traverses the river. Arrive at the 'Old' Dee Bridge. This is probably Roman in origin although the structure that we see today dates from the 14th century. Up to the 19th century it was the only bridge crossing the river to give access to the city.

At this point you have a choice of routes. If you wish to circumnavigate the city walls follow section 2 below; otherwise, go straight to section 3.

75

2. Do not cross the river but turn right and pass under Bridgegate. This gate, medieval in origin, guarded the approach to Chester from North Wales. Straight ahead is Lower Bridge Street, which is rich in architectural splendour. On the left is the Bear and Billet Hotel, a fine example of a 17th-century, black-and-white timber building. Opposite are splendid Georgian houses – one of which is owned by Granada TV News.

Ascend steps at the side of Bridgegate which give access to the city walls. The walls can be walked in any direction but the following account describes an anti-clockwise route, that is, with the river on your right at first.

The walls shortly climb away from the river and turn in a northerly direction. Shortly after passing a renovated Roman hypocaust you arrive at Newgate, which takes the walls over Little St John Street. One of the largest Roman amphitheatres yet discovered has been excavated just outside the walls here.

The walls now wind past more modern buildings and lead past the remains of Thimbleby's Tower to Eastgate, where a narrow bridge, topped by an ornate Victorian clock, passes over Chester's main shopping street. This street contains the famous Rows – two tiers of shops where the top tier is protected by an overhang which forms a protective balcony. Pass close to the cathedral. During the course of this walk there are many places where you can leave the walls and take a closer look at a place of interest before continuing – Chester Cathedral is one of these places.

The cathedral and its environs are most interesting. Standing on the site of a Saxon church, the present building dates from the 11th century. Previously an abbey, it became the Cathedral of the See of Chester in 1541, and has remained so ever since. A detailed account of its long and varied history is available inside.

At the north-east corner of the walls is King Charles Tower. A tablet set into this tower says: 'King Charles stood on this tower September 24th 1645 and saw his army defeated on Rowton Moor'.

The walls now swing to the west where they run high above the Shropshire Union Canal. As Northgate is approached the Bluecoat Hospital can be seen over to the right. A close look reveals a Bluecoat Boy standing over the entrance door reading a book. The walls gradually descend from Northgate, and lead past Morgans Mount, a small watch-tower from which there is a fine view. If the day is clear the Welsh Hills can be seen straight ahead. The walls traverse the new ring-

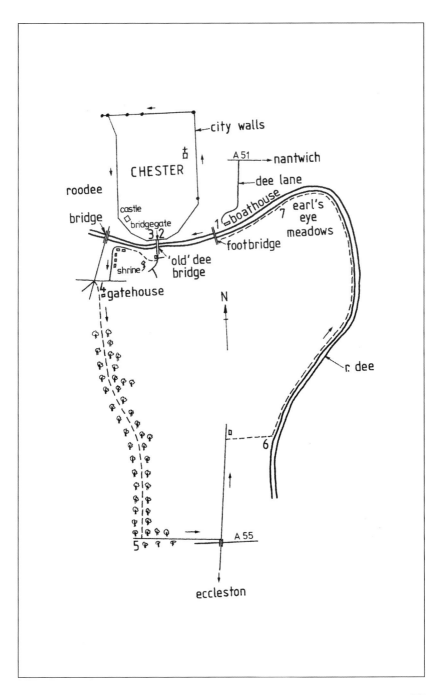

The 17th-century pub at the start of the walk.

road and lead to the Goblin Tower. Originally completely round when first erected during the 13th century, more recent renovations have left this tower a rather odd semicircular shape.

At the north-west corner of the wall stands Bonewaldesthorne Tower. This tower stands close to where the river once flowed, and as the waters gradually receded due to silting, a second tower was built at a lower level. This second tower is called the Water Tower, and the two towers are connected by a flight of steps. At the base of these towers, and outside the walls, there is an attractive parkland setting.

The walls now head southwards and descend to road level. Keep forward and pass in front of the Royal Infirmary, which dates from 1761. Pass the fine old Georgian houses of Stanley Place and then climb over Watergate to continue where the walls run parallel with Nun's Road. Over to the right is the Roodee, where horse racing has been held since 1512. The remains of an old cross can still be seen protruding from the meadow.

The route now crosses Grosvenor Road and runs parallel with Castle Drive. On the left is Chester Castle. A Saxon stronghold once stood on this site, but the present castle contains a contrasting mixture of medieval and 19th-century buildings. The large stone arch of Grosvenor Bridge comes into view over to the right. This fine structure

78

carries the road to Wales over the river Dee. Shortly after passing County Hall arrive back at Bridgegate and the 'Old' Dee Bridge.

3. Cross the fine medieval stone bridge which has seen generations of Handbridge fishermen net the famous Dee salmon as they negotiate the nearby weir which leads them to higher waters. Turn right opposite Mill Street to enter a park. Keep forward along a facing macadam path. On the left shortly, there is a shrine to the Roman goddess Minerva which was carved almost 1,900 years ago into the walls of a quarry.

Leave the park and enter a facing track which commences to the right of a row of houses. The track becomes a lane and takes you past dwellings. Immediately on passing a dwelling called Two Bridges follow the lane as it turns to the left. Gently climb past dwellings on the left and a cemetery on the right. Arrive at a crossing road. Cross the road, taking care, and turn right to follow the roadside pavement.

4. After 200 yards turn left and then left again to pass through large ornate gates which lead onto a facing driveway. Originally built as a direct link to the Duke of Westminster's ancestral home at Eaton Hall, the drive was severed by the construction of the A55 Chester bypass and we are very fortunate indeed to be allowed concessionary access to it. Keep along the main drive, which passes through a parkland setting, for 1½ miles, to arrive at a T-junction.

5. Turn left and follow a narrow lane which stays parallel with the A55. Arrive at a crossing road through a gate. Cross the road, taking care, and turn left to follow the roadside pavement. After ½ mile, and just before the first dwelling on the right is reached, go through a kissing-gate on the right which is virtually opposite a sign which indicates the limits of the City of Chester. Descend to the edge of the river Dee and turn left to pass through a kissing-gate.

6. Follow a well-defined riverside path and negotiate a number of kissing-gates and footbridges. On the approaches to the city there are numerous attractive dwellings on the opposite bank. The river gently bears to the left. This area is called Earl's Eye Meadows and is a haven for all sorts of wildlife.

7. Pass through a kissing-gate at the side of a larger gate and follow a

paved footpath to arrive at, and then cross, a large suspension footbridge which traverses the river. The bridge, which was originally constructed in 1852 but rebuilt in 1923, is an elegant piece of engineering design and connects Queen's Park with The Groves.

A few more strides take you back to the car.

PLACES OF INTEREST

The Deeside village of *Eccleston* is well worth a visit. In order to get there, drive in a southerly direction away from the 'Old' Dee Bridge at Chester, and follow the signs to Eccleston, which is 2 miles away.

The pride of the village is the magnificent sandstone church, which is surrounded by dwellings, all of which have neat, well-tended gardens. A visit to the church leads through a pair of splendid gates, and on down an avenue of trees, planted in 1935 to commemorate the Silver Jubilee of King George V and Queen Mary. Members of the house of Grosvenor, Dukes of Westminster, are buried in the church, and their family home, Eaton Hall, lies only a mile away across the fields.

Strolling by the Dee

BEESTON AND THE SHROPSHIRE UNION CANAL

Throughout this walk, which takes in a most attractive stretch of the Shropshire Union Canal, you are virtually always in sight of two castles. There are also long views to the ridges of the Peckforton and Bickerton Hills. An added attraction is that the route takes you past an 'ice cream farm', where 30 different flavours of ice creams and sorbets can be sampled.

The Shropshire Union Canal

The central Cheshire Plain is dominated by three physical features in the landscape: the Bickerton Hills and the Peckforton Hills together with an adjacent rock which is topped by the ruins of Beeston Castle. Peckforton can also boast a castle, built for the first Lord Tollemache during the years 1844 to 1850. It therefore has little historical significance but, nevertheless, its outward appearance is all that a castle should be, and its imposing towers and battlements are in complete contrast to the ruins of Beeston which has a much longer and more varied, history. Built by Rannulf de Blunderville, seventh Earl of Chester, during the early 13th century, the castle played an important role during the Civil War, being captured by the Royalists in 1645. Early the next year, following their eventual victory, the Parliamentarian forces destroyed the greater part of the castle. Although now in ruins, a mental picture can be built up of how it must have looked when in its prime and the views from the summit of the rock on which the castle stands are superb.

The Shady Oak inn is on Bates Mill Lane to the north of Beeston Castle. The inn is on the route of the walk and is pleasantly situated by the Shropshire Union Canal. In recent years, it has been etended to provide a large open plan dining area where a good selection of tempting dishes can be eaten in attractive surroundings. There are starters, main courses, grills, a vegetarian slection, filled jacket potatoes, sandwiches and baguettes, as well as a comprehensive menu for children. To finish off, there are sweets, puddings and a cheese board. The Shady Oak serves a comprehensive range of ales and cider as well as a good selection of wines. There is a large conservatory, a canal-side beer garden and a children's play area and the inn is open every day from 11.30 am, with meals served every day between 11.30 am and 9 pm. Telephone: 01829 730718.

- HOW TO GET THERE: The A49 connects Warrington and Whitchurch. The village of Beeston lies one mile to the west of this road, 11 miles to the north of Whitchurch. If you wish to start the walk from the Shady Oak inn, drive along Bates Mill Lane, which commences on the northern side of Beeston Castle, and after crossing the canal arrive at the inn.
- PARKING: There is a Sandstone Trail car park and picnic site about 100 yards from the entrance gate of Beeston Castle. Alternatively, if you are visiting the castle, you may leave the car in a car park which is opposite the entrance gate.
- LENGTH OF THE WALK: 7 miles. Map: OS Landranger 117 Chester (GR 540590).

THE WALK

1. On leaving the Sandstone Trail car park turn left, and then left again, to follow the Sandstone Trail through trees to a crossing lane. Turn right along the lane and pass Castleside Farm and another

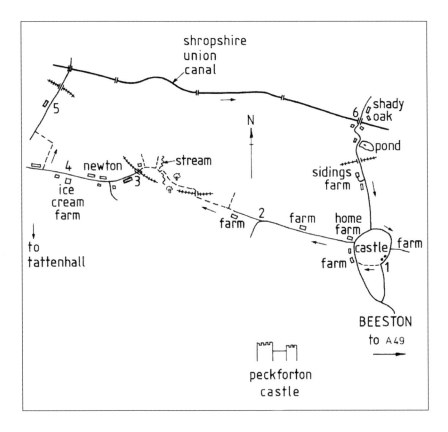

dwelling. Arrive at a junction close by Home Farm. Turn left here, in the direction of Burwardsley and Tattenhall. Keep on past Lower Rock Farm to where, about ¼ mile further on, the lane turns sharply to the left.

2. Leave the lane here, to enter a facing narrow lane, which is headed by a No Through Road sign. On reaching a farm, the lane becomes a track. Keep forward now, past a track which goes off to the right, and shortly pass over the railway via a bridge. The track stays parallel with the railway for a couple of hundred yards and then gently bears away to the right. The track becomes a grassy path. At a point where the track meets a stream turn left over a stone flag bridge and cross a stile to enter a rough field. Turn right and, after only 20 yards, go over a stile in a crossing fence. There is a junction of ways now, where a narrow track goes off to the right, but ignore this and keep forward

83

A glimpse of Peckforton Castle through the trees.

along the main track. Arrive at a junction of tracks where a dwelling can be seen straight ahead.

3. Keep forward here, to pass under a bridge which carries the railway overhead. The way is now along a facing macadam lane, which leads past a row of cottages. Arrive at a junction of lanes and turn right. Pass Rose Cottage, Yew Tree Farm and Newton Grange. Pass other dwellings and, after further 250 yards, arrive at Cheshire Ice Cream Farm.

Apart from Christmas and New Year the premises are open every day and provide an opportunity to view how ice cream is made – and free samples are available! There is also a small café where a range of home-made snacks can be purchased.

4. Having sampled the ice cream, continue along the lane. Pass a couple of dwellings and then arrive at a row of houses on the right. Do not walk past these houses but turn right to pass over a stile at the side of a field gate just before them. Enter a field and walk forward, keeping the garden fence of the first house on your immediate left. Where the fence finishes, keep forward and walk straight across the facing field. About 30 yards before arriving at a crossing hedgerow, turn left and

The Shady Oak, near Beeston

gradually converge with the hedge to arrive at the field corner where a stile takes you onto a crossing road. Turn right.

5. Follow the road over the railway. After a further 150 yards, leave the road, to the right, just before the canal bridge, and turn right to walk along the towpath of the Shropshire Union Canal.

From Chester, the Shropshire Union Canal goes through Christleton, and then passes close to Tattenhall, on its route to Nantwich and Audlem, after which it enters the county of Shropshire.

Follow this attractive stretch of waterway for 2½ miles, passing under three bridges en route.

6. Leave the towpath at bridge number 109 to enter a lane. On the left here, is the Shady Oak Inn, where refreshment can be taken. The route continues to the right to follow a lane which turns sharply between dwellings. On the left now there is a large ornamental pond, with islands, the home of many different species of wildfowl. The lane leads over the railway and past Sidings Farm and other dwellings.

Straight ahead there is a fine view of the precipitous rock on which the ruin of Beeston Castle sits.

85

On arriving at a T-junction turn left and follow a lane where the perimeter wall which surrounds the castle site is on your immediate right. Keep on, past Castle Gate Farm and a single track road which goes off to the left, to shortly arrive back at the car park.

PLACES OF INTEREST

The twin castles of *Beeston* and *Peckforton* are both very interesting and well worth visiting.

Beeston Castle is open daily between 10 am and 6 pm from April to September inclusive. During the winter months the opening hours are 10 am to 4 pm. Telephone: 0191 261 1585.

Peckforton Castle, whose fine silhouette has been used in the making of several historical dramas, is open Monday to Thursday throughout the year. You can explore its main building, battlements and perimeter moat walk – but it should be noted that the surrounding lands are not under the ownership of the castle. Telephone: 01829 260930.

THE TRENT AND MERSEY CANAL AT HASSALL GREEN

From Hassall Green, the walk takes you along the towpath of the Trent and Mersey Canal. The route then turns away from the canal to cross the rich agricultural countryside of south-east Cheshire before returning to Hassall Green along paths and lanes.

The Trent and Mersey Canal

Long before the M6 motorway bisected the village of Hassall Green, the construction of another highway had caused exactly the same effect. This was the Trent and Mersey Canal – which was completed in 1777. The canal, which is 93 miles in length, runs from the Bridgewater Canal near Runcorn to the river Trent at Shardlow. From Runcorn, the Cheshire section of the canal goes through Preston Brook and past Northwich to Middlewich, before climbing out of the Cheshire Plain through 35 locks, known to the boat people as 'Heartbreak Hill'. The canal was engineered by James Brindley, who called it the 'Grand

'Trunk' and looked upon other navigations as mere branches. Unfortunately, Brindley died five years before the canal was completed, when responsibility for construction was taken over by his brother-in-law, Hugh Henshall. It is hard to believe that the canal was completed at a total cost of £300,000 – money which, today, would only purchase a few hundred yards of the nearby M6 motorway.

The Romping Donkey, which is a Tetley's house, is a pleasant place to enjoy a meal and a drink. Built during the early part of the 17th century, the inn was a welcome refreshment stop for the early 'bargees' on the nearby canal. There is a beamed bar and separate lounge where a wide selection of bar meals are served every lunchtime and during the evening. You will find a large garden with trestle tables and benches at the front of the inn, which can be used when the weather is fine. Telephone: 01270 765202.

- HOW TO GET THERE: The village of Hassall Green lies just off the A533 Sandbach to Alsager road close by the M6 motorway.
- PARKING: The Romping Donkey inn has a large car park (for patrons). Alternatively, there is a car park at the commencement of the 'Salt Line' – which is a little further on from the inn close to where the motorway crosses the lane.
- LENGTH OF THE WALK: 4 miles. Map: OS Landranger 118 Stoke-on-Trent (GR 779584).

THE WALK

1. From the Romping Donkey, turn left, in the direction of Hassall and Wheelock, to where after 150 yards, the lane crosses the Trent and Mersey Canal. Cross the canal and turn right to descend onto its towpath. Pass a set of locks and follow the towpath under the M6 motorway. Pass under bridge number 148 and continue past another set of locks. About 300 yards further on, pass a set of locks and go under a bridge. Immediately on passing the next set of locks go under bridge number 150. Shortly after the next set of locks the towpath bridges a short inlet arm of the canal. Arrive at another set of locks, where there is a row of cottages on the left. There is a bridge now (number 151). Do not walk under this bridge, but leave the towpath here, through a gap in a wall on the left.

2. Turn right and then left, to follow a track past dwellings called White Cottage and Mount Croft. Go through a gap at the side of a

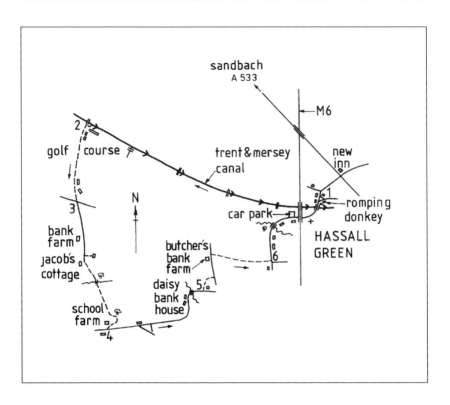

facing gate to enter a golf course. Keep forward along the main path which descends, takes you over a stream, and then climbs. Go through a gap at the side of a facing gate and continue along a track which takes you past dwellings. Arrive at a crossing road.

3. Go over the road to enter a facing lane where a sign points to Hassall Moss. Pass Bank Farm and descend. At the bottom of the descent keep forward past Jacob's Cottage and climb steps to go over a stile which takes you into an undulating field. Bear left now, and climb a few yards over rising ground. Straight ahead, about ¼ mile away, a farm can be seen on the skyline. Walk in the direction of the farm and gradually descend across the field. Go over a stile at the side of a hedgerow and immediately cross a stream via a narrow footbridge. Go over a second stile and then aim to the left of the farm on the skyline. On reaching the field corner go over two stiles in quick succession. Climb up the next field, bearing left, to go over a stile which is about 60 yards to the left of the farm outbuildings at the

St Philip's – the 'Pink' church.

base of a large tree. Walk forward now, where there is a fence on the right, and then turn right to pass over two stiles in quick succession. Arrive on a lane close by the entrance to School Farm and Willow Barn.

4. Turn left along the lane. Keep on the main lane and follow it as it descends and turns to left and right past Lodley Smithy and the adjacent Daisy Bank House. About 80 yards further on, leave the lane to the left, over a stile, just before a dwelling is reached.

5. Follow a field edge, keeping the garden hedgerow of the dwelling on your immediate right and follow it as it turns to the right. Pass over a stile at the side of a gate and arrive on a lane. Turn left and gradually climb along the lane. Shortly after passing Butcher's Bank Farm go over a stile on the right, immediately cross a second stile, and keep forward to follow a field edge, where there is a hedgerow on the right. Cross another stile and keep on in the same direction as before with a fence now on the right. Pass an isolated stile and emerge onto a crossing lane over a stile at the side of a gate. There is a junction here, where Hassall Road commences.

6. Turn left now and keep along the laneside verge to gradually

descend past a dwelling on the right called Hillside (1910). The lane takes you over a stream and then past the car park for the 'Salt Line'. Pass under the M6 motorway. On the right here is the delightful pink-painted building of St Philip's church. Arrive at the bridge which takes you over the Trent and Mersey Canal.

The Romping Donkey inn is 150 yards away, straight ahead.

PLACES OF INTEREST

Less than 3 miles from Hassall Green, and accessible via the A533, is the ancient town of *Sandbach*. Its main feature is a delightful cobbled market place where historic buildings overlook two richly carved Anglo-Saxon sandstone crosses, which date from between the 8th and 9th centuries. Apart from the crosses, there are numerous black-and-white timbered buildings, old inns and interesting shops to explore.

MOW COP AND THE MACCLESFIELD CANAL

From Scholar Green, the walk takes in a picturesque section of the Macclesfield Canal before a steep climb along tracks and woodland paths to Mow Cop village. The route goes past 'The Old Man of Mow' and Mow Cop Folly before descending along lanes, tracks and paths back to Scholar Green.

Looking over the Cheshire Plain from near Mow Cop Folly.

At 1,100 feet above sea level and on the Cheshire-Staffordshire border, Mow Cop dominates the landscape to the south of Congleton.

The vistas across the surrounding countryside are stunning and at least six counties can be seen from Mow Cop Folly – a tower built on an outcrop of rock at the rear of the village. Running around the base of the hill on which Mow Cop is situated is the Macclesfield Canal, heading north past the outskirts of Congleton on its way to Macclesfield and Marple. This elevated section of the canal provides a platform for long views across the Cheshire Plain. The canal would have been utilised for the transport of sandstone, which was quarried in the Mow Cop area from the time of the Romans, and the cut-out shapes of millstones can still be seen in the now abandoned quarries.

Just to the west of Mow Cop, in Scholar Green, the Rising Sun is a local village freehouse which has, during recent times, been extensively renovated – resulting in a hostelry of charm and character. The inn serves a range of Marston's, Robinson's and Tetley beers, together with draught cider. Meals are available both at lunchtime and during the evening and traditional Sunday lunches are a speciality. All dishes are freshly prepared and home-cooked, using fresh local produce when available. The extensive menu is frequently changed and visitors would be hard pressed not to discover dishes which suited their tastes. Accompanied children are made welcome in the dining room up to 8 pm in the evening. Telephone: 01782 776235.

- HOW TO GET THERE: The walk commences at the Rising Sun inn at Scholar Green. The bulk of the village lies to the east of the A34, midway between Congleton and Newcastle-under-Lyme, about one mile to the north of the junction between the A34 and the A50. The Rising Sun is about ½ mile from the A34, in the direction of Mow Cop, close to where Station Road crosses the Macclesfield Canal.
- PARKING: There is a car park at the Rising Sun (for patrons). Alternatively, there is a parking layby on Station Road between the A34 and the inn.

    There is also a car park at Mow Cop Folly – which can be seen on the skyline and is signposted from Scholar Green. You would then start the walk at point 5.
- LENGTH OF THE WALK: 5 miles. Map: OS Landranger 118 Stoke-on-Trent (GR 837575).

THE WALK

1. From the Rising Sun, turn right and after only 100 yards arrive at a bridge which crosses the Macclesfield Canal. Turn right here and descend onto the canal towpath. Walk under the bridge, which is number 87, and continue along the towpath. After a couple of hundred yards there is a marina on the opposite side of the canal.

The Macclesfield Canal joins the Trent and Mersey Canal about 2 miles from Scholar Green. The canal passes Congleton and then climbs over 100 feet through a series of locks at Bosley, prior to

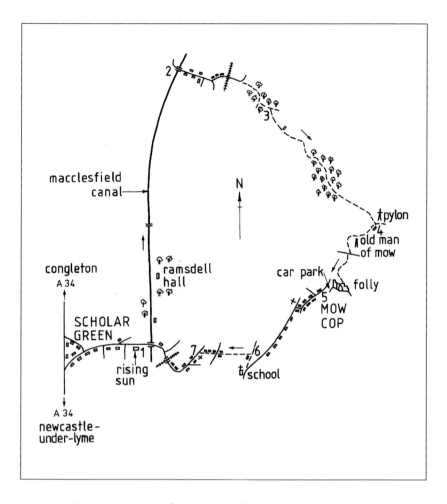

running through Macclesfield and Bollington to join the Peak Forest Canal at Marple.

There are long views over to the left now, across acres of lush, green, wooded countryside. Shortly, over to the right, can be seen the splendid 18th-century mansion of Ramsdell Hall where graceful lawns sweep down to the canalside.

Pass under bridge number 86 and after a further ½ mile, arrive at bridge number 85.

2. Walk under the bridge and turn left to leave the canal towpath. Join New Road and turn left to walk across the bridge. Pass dwellings, to

94

where, shortly after passing a telephone box, there is a junction. Turn left here, to enter Yew Tree Lane. Pass bungalows and arrive at the railway. Go through a kissing-gate on the right and pass through a tunnel which takes you under the rail tracks. Go through another kissing-gate and turn right to follow a hedged-in lane. After 80 yards there is a fork. Keep forward here, along a facing track which gradually climbs towards trees. The track turns to the right. About 80 yards further on, there is a junction of ways. Keep left here to climb along the main track and after a further 100 yards fork right to go through a small gate at the side of a field gate.

3. Climb forward now, to follow a grassy path up an undulating field. A dwelling comes into view. Pass to the right of its garden hedgerow and continue to climb, where there is a fence on the immediate left. Turn right shortly, just before the fence finishes, to follow the edge of a gully. Climb towards a wood and then go over a stile on the left between a holly bush and a low stone wall. The path quickly turns to the right and climbs for quite a way through trees. Go over a stile and emerge from the trees. Straight ahead, a pylon can be seen on a facing hilltop. Walk in the direction of the pylon and follow a field edge, keeping a fence, and then a wall, on your immediate right. Go through a gate at the field corner and keep along the edge of the next field.

There are long views across to the left here where the mast on top of Croker Hill can be seen which is 8 miles away.

Cross a stile and follow the path to a junction of ways.

4. Turn right now, to follow a level track past a dwelling. The track is a platform for marvellous views across the Cheshire Plain, which stretches out below as far as the eye can see.

On the left shortly, there is a large splinter of rock which is known as 'The Old Man of Mow'. Almost 70 feet tall, the rock is so named because it is said to resemble a human head and was left in its solitary position after the surrounding rock was quarried away.

The track winds and leads to a crossing lane. Turn right here, and then left, to follow a track which takes you to Mow Cop Folly. Steps lead up to the building, which is now ruinous.

The Folly, built in 1754, was originally a summer house used by its owner, one Randle Wilbraham of Rode Hall, who could look out from his house 2½ miles away to his creation on the skyline. If the day is clear the views from here are superb. To the north is Macclesfield

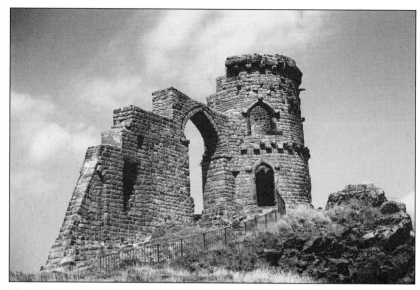

The ruins of Mow Cop Folly.

Forest and Alderley Edge; to the north-west the radio telescope at Jodrell Bank; to the west Beeston Castle and the Welsh Hills; to the south-west the Shropshire Hills; to the south the Potteries dominate the landscape, whilst to the east is Biddulph Moor with the Peak District beyond. At this point you are at the very limit of the county boundary and only a few yards from Staffordshire.

At the base of the rock on which Mow Cop Folly stands there is a car park.

5. From the car park turn left to follow a lane past dwellings. Keep on, past Top Station Road, and at the next junction turn right at the village shop and post office. Arrive at a junction virtually opposite Mow Cop Methodist Church. Turn left here, along Woodcock Lane, and descend. There are dwellings on the left and open fields on the right. On reaching Church Street, which turns to the left, turn right to enter Halls Road. Follow a macadam lane which quickly becomes a rough track.

6. Immediately on passing a bungalow leave the track to the left along a path which descends between fences. Cross a stile and descend along the next field edge where there is a fence on the immediate left.

Pass over a stile at the field corner and follow a fenced-in path to a track between houses. Walk straight over a crossing road, taking care, to enter a facing lane where there are dwellings on the right and fields on the left. The lane becomes a track and leads to a crossing road called The Bank.

7. Turn left to pass Bank Methodist Church. Follow the roadside pavement past cottages and keep on past Mill Lane. The road turns to the right shortly, at which point the pavement is on the opposite side. Gradually descend along the roadside and pass under the railway to arrive at a junction. Keep left here, where a sign tells you that Scholar Green is ½ mile away.

Cross the canal and arrive back at the Rising Sun.

PLACES OF INTEREST

Just over one mile to the north of Scholar Green, on the A34 road towards Congleton, is the magnificent black-and-white building of *Little Moreton Hall*. The moated Hall, which was the ancestral home of the Moreton family until acquired by the National Trust in 1937, has been little altered since it was constructed during the late 15th and early 16th centuries. It is claimed by many to be the most popular of all English black-and-white houses, a boast supported by the numerous calendars in which it appears. The hall is open to the public from late March (closed Good Friday) to the end of September, every afternoon except Monday and Tuesday. Telephone: 01260 272018.

THE SHROPSHIRE UNION CANAL AT BARBRIDGE

The first section of the walk follows the Middlewich Branch of the Shropshire Union Canal, after which the route turns south across field paths and lanes to join the towpath of the main course of the canal to the south of Hurleston Junction. The return leg then follows the canal back to Barbridge.

Barbridge Junction

The tiny village of Barbridge is well known to those who spend their leisure time cruising along the waters of the Shropshire Union Canal. There is a junction of canal routes here, where a branch of the canal heads off to Middlewich to join the Trent and Mersey Canal. Many years ago, the main road between Nantwich and Chester used to run through the village. However, the main road now runs to the west of the village centre, which has created a more tranquil atmosphere. The village contains a mixture of dwellings – many of which are situated by the water's edge, and there is a fine inn, the Barbridge, where the boat-people can enjoy a hearty meal whilst relating their adventures to fellow travellers.

The inn has a roomy interior, with a separate dining area – which overlooks the canal, and contains maps and paintings associated with the waterway. Popular with canal-users and locals alike, a wide-ranging menu of delicious home-cooked food is served throughout the day. To complement the food the bar serves hand-pulled cask ales, and guest beers are available in the summertime. There is a large canalside garden, a children's play area, and barbecues are regularly served during the summer months. Telephone: 01270 528443.

- HOW TO GET THERE: The A51 runs between Nantwich and Chester. Barbridge straddles this road 4 miles to the north-west of Nantwich.
- PARKING: On the eastern side of the A51 the Old Chester Road runs parallel with the Shropshire Union Canal. There is good roadside parking available here, on the left-hand side of the road, about 100 yards before the Barbridge Inn. Alternatively, if you are using the facilities of the inn, you may park there.
- LENGTH OF THE WALK: 8 miles. Map: OS Landranger 118 Stoke-on-Trent (GR 616566).

THE WALK

1. On leaving the car, walk over bridge 100 (which spans the canal about 100 yards from the inn) and immediately turn right to descend onto the towpath of the canal. Turn right and pass under the bridge you have just walked across to shortly pass the Barbridge Inn, which is on the opposite side of the canal. Join a lane which takes you over a bridge, where the Jolly Tar inn can be seen over to the left. Immediately on passing over the bridge descend to the left to rejoin the canal towpath. Turn sharply to the left here, to pass under the bridge you have just walked across.

2. This is Barbridge Junction where the Middlewich Branch leaves the main course of the Shropshire Union Canal. Keep along the Middlewich Branch towpath and pass under three bridges to arrive at a lock. Walk under bridge 5. On the right now, there is a large marina (with a tea-room attached). Continue along the towpath and pass under a bridge which carries the Crewe to Chester railway line over the canal. The canal is arrow-straight now for about ¾ mile, and is

99

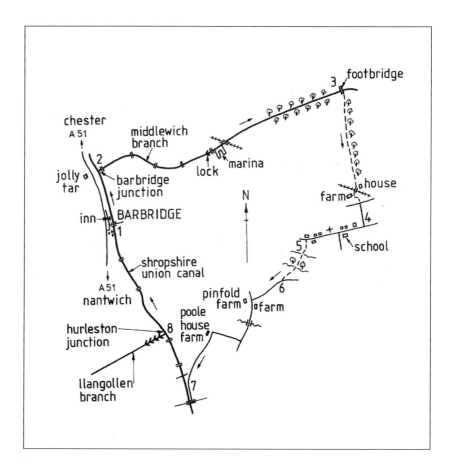

shortly tree-lined. Where the straight section finishes there is a footbridge which gently arches over the canal. Leave the towpath here and climb to the left to pass over a fence-stile. Go over another stile which gives access to the footbridge.

3. Cross the footbridge and then go over a stile to enter a field. Keep forward here, along the field edge, where there are hawthorn trees on the immediate left. After 250 yards cross a stile at the side of a gate and keep on, in the same general direction as before. Arrive at a facing gate and go over a stile on the left to follow a well-defined track between widely-spaced hedgerows. Pass over another stile at the side of a gate and follow a short length of concrete drive. A stile on the left gives access to a bridge which takes you over the railway. Immediately on

The canalside inn at Barbridge.

crossing the bridge go through a small gate on the left which gives access to a hedged-in track. The track skirts around a farm and leads to a crossing road. Walk straight over the crossing road to enter a straight length of facing lane. Arrive at a T junction of lanes.

4. Turn right now, to pass Worleston House and other dwellings. Immediately on passing Worleston Primary School there is a junction of lanes where Barons Road goes off to the left. Keep forward here, to enter Church Road. Pass St Oswald's church and then keep on past Maple House and West View, to where, about ¼ mile after passing the church, there are semi-detached dwellings on the right. The first of these dwellings is called Hillcrest.

5. Leave the lane to the left now, opposite the entrance drive of the second dwelling, and cross a plank-bridge and stile to enter a field. Go over a narrow section of the facing field to where, after only 50 yards, you pass over a pair of stiles at the right hand side of a telegraph pole. You have now entered a very large, undulating field. Walk forward, bearing right, away from the hedgerow on the left, aiming to the right of an electricity pylon, which can be seen across the field. On arriving at a crossing hedgerow, go over a pair of stiles at either end of a

101

The Shropshire Union Canal

footbridge, which takes you over a stream and into a field. Bear slightly right now and walk under overhead cables towards trees at the far side of the field. A stream meanders through the trees. Go over a footbridge here, and then turn right to go over a stile which is about 60 yards away at the side of a gate. You have now entered a very large field. Follow a facing gravel track and cross the field to arrive at a gate. Go through the gate to emerge onto a lane.

6. Turn right along the lane. In about ½ mile, the lane leads to a T-junction where a sign tells you that it is called Poole Old Hall Lane. Turn left now, pass The Pinfold Farm Centre, and gradually descend to follow the lane over a stone bridge. About 200 yards further on, turn right, to enter Poole Hill Road; although called a 'road' it is a typical remote country lane which meanders between hedgerows. After ¼ mile, the lane turns sharply to the left opposite the delightful Georgian building of Poole House Farm. After a further ½ mile, the lane runs parallel with the Shropshire Union Canal, which is on the immediate right.

7. Leave the lane here and turn right along the canal towpath. Pass under a pipe-main which is carried over the canal. Pass under a couple

of bridges and arrive at Hurleston Junction. To the left is the Llangollen Branch of the canal, which commences with a series of locks.

8. Keep forward now, to continue along the towpath in the direction of Chester. On the left, here, is the raised banking of Hurleston Reservoir. The final mile of the walk takes you through some lush, green countryside. Pass under bridges 98 and 99 to arrive back at bridge 100, close to where you commenced your journey.

PLACES OF INTEREST
Only 4 miles to the south-east of Barbridge, and directly accessible via the A51 road, is the old market town of *Nantwich*, famous for its fine half-timbered buildings and beautiful church. The Nantwich Museum on Pillory Street is well worth a visit for it gives an insight into the life and times of this historic market town. There are Roman exhibits, a Civil War display, early photographs and an exhibition of Cheshire cheesemaking. The museum is open Tuesday to Saturday between 10.30 am and 4.30 pm. Telephone: 01270 627104.

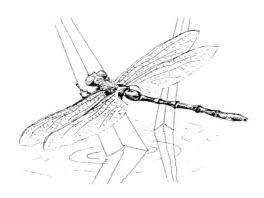

FARNDON AND THE RIVER DEE

Commencing at picturesque Farndon, the walk will take you along tracks, paths and lanes to the outskirts of the village of Churton before returning along a scenic path which follows the course of the winding river Dee.

The river Dee at Farndon

The village of Farndon is, quite literally, a stone's throw from Wales. The majority of its dwellings are perched on a prominence overlooking the river Dee, and a famous medieval bridge links it to its Welsh counterpart, the village of Holt.

There must have been a crossing place at this point on the river from early times, for Farndon lies on a Roman road. Probably a ford or ferry was used initially, followed by the construction of a wooden bridge – which itself was superseded by a stone bridge on which building work began during 1345. For travellers to and from Wales, Farndon was a popular watering hole and overnight stopping place during the days when horse-drawn coaches were the main means of long-distance travel.

The village has a place in English history for it was at Farndon during AD 925 that King Edward, known as 'the Elder', who was the son of Alfred the Great, died after dealing with rebellious Welsh tribes. Following his death his body was taken to Winchester for burial.

There are still many attractive black-and-white dwellings in the village, predominantly in High Street and Church Lane, many in High Street still retaining their thatched roofs. The village has three inns and an interesting church dedicated to St Chad.

The Greyhound Inn in the centre of the village is open for meals every evening, and at lunch time on Saturday and all day Sunday. There is a board proclaiming special dishes and vegetarians are well catered for. The range of liquid refreshment includes four real ales and four cask ales – together with various lagers and ciders. The inn has an attractive open-plan lounge which makes for a welcoming atmosphere. Telephone 01829 270244.

- HOW TO GET THERE: The A534 connects the Welsh town of Wrexham with Nantwich. Farndon straddles this road about 6 miles from Wrexham at a point where it crosses the river Dee and enters England.
- PARKING: There is a car park, for patrons, at the rear of the Greyhound Inn. Alternatively, there is a riverside car park (and toilets) close by the bridge which links Farndon with Holt.
- LENGTH OF THE WALK: 5 miles. Map: OS Landranger 117 Chester (GR 412546).

THE WALK

1. From the Greyhound Inn, follow the roadside pavement to gently climb past Churton Road and Church Street. Keep on, past Barnston Court and Lloyd Close, to where, immediately after passing a row of thatched black-and-white dwellings, the aptly named Walkers Lane goes off to the left.

2. Enter Walkers Lane, which initially takes you between dwellings. The lane becomes a hedged-in track and leads to a kissing-gate. Go through the gate and emerge into a large field. Keep forward along the field edge where there is a hedgerow on the immediate left. Over to the right there are long views across to the Peckforton Hills.

Go through a metal kissing-gate at the field corner and across the next field to go through another kissing-gate. There is now a

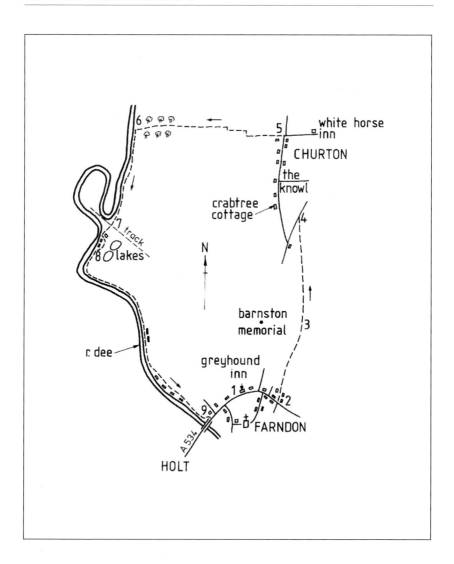

hedgerow on the immediate right. Where the hedgerow finishes, keep forward through a gap in the same general direction as before, to cross a large field.

Over to the left here can be seen the needle-sharp structure of the Barnston Memorial – built to commemorate the gallant actions of a local soldier, Major Roger Barnston, at the Relief of Lucknow in 1857.

3. Having crossed the field keep on and pass through a gap. There is a

hedgerow on the immediate right for a short distance, after which the path leads across a field, to once again continue with a hedgerow on the immediate right. The hedgerow turns away to the right after 100 yards but keep on to pass through a metal kissing-gate which is set in a crossing hedgerow. Bear very slightly left now and cross a large field to gradually converge with a hedgerow on the left which has a metal kissing-gate set into it.

4. Go through the kissing-gate, cross a road, and turn left to follow the roadside pavement. After 180 yards turn sharp right to enter Stannage Lane. Pass Crabtree Cottage and keep on past The Knowl to arrive at a staggered junction (the White Horse Inn at the heart of the village of Churton is 180 yards along the lane to the right).

5. Turn left at the staggered junction to follow a rough grassy track between hedges and trees. Gradually descend along the track. The track winds, then continues with a large holly hedge on the right. Pass over a stile at the side of a facing gate and follow an obvious grassy track which takes you into trees by the edge of the river Dee.

6. Turn left along a riverside track which becomes a path. Emerge from the trees through a kissing-gate and continue along the riverside.
    At this point the Dee forms the boundary between England and Wales.
    Follow the edge of two large fields and pass through gates to arrive at a crossing track where the river turns away to the right.

7. Walk straight across the track, pass through a metal kissing-gate, then follow the edge of a rough field. Arrive at the riverside once again and turn left to pass through two gates. Follow a gravel track now which turns to the right at the rear of dwellings. On the left here there are a couple of small lakes. After 80 yards turn right up steps to follow a short section of fenced-in path. Pass through a kissing-gate and keep along the riverside once again.

8. For the next 1½ miles follow a well-worn path which never strays far from the riverside and go through a number of gates. There are quite a few weekend dwellings along this section of the route. Arrive at the stone bridge which connects Farndon with Holt.
    It is known that work on the bridge began during 1345 and, apart

The 14th-century bridge across the Dee at Farndon.

from Chester bridge, it is the only surviving medieval bridge in Cheshire. During the Civil War (1642–49) there were many skirmishes at the bridge, for the river Dee was the dividing point between Parliamentarian Cheshire and Royalist North Wales.

9. Leave the riverside to the left of the bridge and gently climb along the roadside pavement back into the village of Farndon.

It would be a pity to conclude the walk at this point without seeing something more of the village; so if time permits enter Church Lane and stroll past picturesque cottages. Turn next left and walk up to the village church, which is dedicated to St Chad. Much of the church was rebuilt following the ravages of the Civil War, at which time an interesting stained-glass window was installed depicting the figures and coats of arms of local families involved in the conflict.

A famous son of Farndon was John Speed, who mapped the counties of England during the 16th century.

Leave the church confines along the path leading directly from the porch entrance, then walk along a facing road at the end of which is a rather fine Georgian building. Turn next left to arrive back at the Greyhound Inn.

PLACES OF INTEREST

A little over 3 miles by road from Farndon there is a lovely old restored water mill which is well worth a visit. To get there drive in an easterly direction away from Farndon along the A534 and after a couple of miles arrive at the village of Barton. Enter a road which begins at the side of the Cock O'Barton inn and after ¾ mile turn left where a sign tells you that *Stretton Water Mill* is ¼ mile away.

There has been a mill at Stretton since the 14th century. The mill was in use until 1959, after which it fell into a state of disrepair. During 1975 it was restored by Cheshire County Council and opened the following year as a working museum. At the time of renovation a small adjacent barn was turned into an exhibition area.

The opening times are from 1 pm to 5 pm every day, except Monday, between April and the end of September (open Bank Holiday Monday afternoons). During March and October the mill is open at weekends (Saturday and Sunday only) between 1 pm and 5 pm. It is closed during the winter months. Telephone for information: 01606 41331.

ACTON AND THE 'SHROPPIE'

This predominantly towpath walk – through some lovely Cheshire countryside – presents an opportunity to stroll along the Llangollen Branch of the 'Shroppie' as well as by the main canal.

Bridge No. 8 on the Shropshire Union Canal.

The approach to Acton is dominated by the 800 year old tower of St Mary's church – around which the final stages of the Battle of Nantwich were fought in 1644 during the Civil War. Originally established by monks from Combermere Abbey near Whitchurch in 1180, the church contains 14th and 17th-century effigies as well as elaborate wooden carvings. The graveyard contains the tomb of Albert Hornby – who was the England cricket captain during the 1882 Test Match against Australia which gave birth to The Ashes. There has been a school at Acton since 1662 and one of its former pupils, Wallace Oakes, was posthumously awarded the George Cross for his bravery in saving hundreds of lives during a railway disaster. There is a village pub, the Star Inn, and a number of delightful cottages.

From Ellesmere Port and then Chester, the Shropshire Union Canal runs in a generally southerly direction passing Nantwich and Audlem – at which point it leaves the county of Cheshire. Three miles to the north-west of Nantwich there is a junction where a branch of the canal leads to Llangollen. The village of Acton is situated between and close to both these waterways.

Less than three miles to the west of Acton, and accessed from the A534 Nantwich to Wrexham road, is the attractive Thatch Inn at Faddiley. The inn is a free house and offers a wide choice of cask conditioned beers – many from private breweries. The range of food is also extensive and there is something to suit every taste. The menu changes from time to time and there are also 'special' dishes to choose from with everything prepared on the premises. There is an attractive beer garden with benches, and families are assured of a friendly welcome. Telephone: 01270 524223.

- HOW TO GET THERE: Acton straddles the A534 Nantwich to Wrexham road a little over one mile to the west of Nantwich.
- PARKING: There is a large free car park in the centre of the village, virtually opposite the Star Inn.
- LENGTH OF THE WALK: 5½ miles. Map: OS Landranger 118 Stoke-on-Trent (GR 633530).

THE WALK

1. From the car park, cross the road and turn left to pass the Star Inn. Enter a track on the right now, which initially stays parallel with the road and takes you through trees. Immediately on passing a dwelling on the left, go through a gap at the side of a gate and then turn right to follow a path across a field. Across to the right there is a fine view of Acton church. Pass over a stile in a crossing fence and follow a well-defined path which leads towards the right-hand side of a farm which can be seen about ¼ mile away.

2. On drawing level with the farmhouse cross a stile and keep to the right of a line of silver birch trees to join the entrance drive of the farm. Follow the drive and after 60 yards arrive at a crossing lane. A sign here tells you that the farm is called Madam's Farm. Walk straight across the lane, go through a gap at the side of a facing gate and cross a field in the same direction as before. Go through a gap in a hedgerow and keep on across the next field, to a stile which can be seen in front of a

111

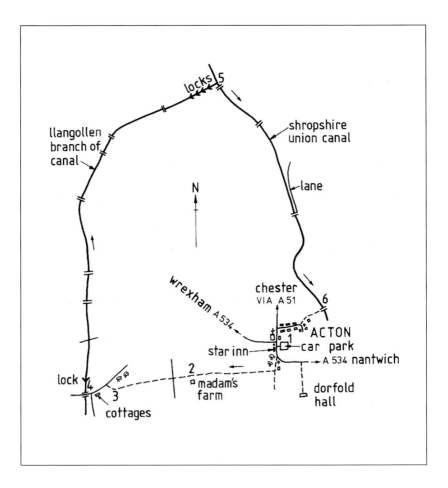

dwelling which is about 250 yards away, straight ahead.

3. Go over a macadam driveway via a pair of stiles and then bear slightly right to cross a field corner. Cross a stile, turn left and follow a road past cottages. Keep on past Swanley Lane – which goes off to the left to Stoneley Green and Ravensmoor – and arrive at a bridge. Do not cross this bridge but descend steps on the left which take you onto a canal towpath.

4. Turn right and follow the towpath under the bridge (number 8) to almost immediately pass a lock. Keep on past Swanley Bridge Marina. You are walking alongside the Llangollen Branch of the Shropshire

The attractive Thatch Inn.

Union Canal. The canal was abandoned to navigation in 1944 but was re-opened a few years later following an extensive clearance operation and its route into Wales is an attractive one for the pleasure boaters of today. Follow the towpath for almost 2 miles, passing under bridges 6, 5, 4, 3, and 2. Immediately on passing under the next twin-bridge arrive at a descending set of four locks. Descend to Hurleston Junction to cross a bridge which takes you onto the towpath of the main course of the Shropshire Union Canal.

5. Turn right, where a sign points towards Birmingham, and keep along the canal towpath.

Often called the 'Shroppie', the canal links Ellesmere Port with Wolverhampton and the Black Country and was, in days gone by, an artery in an extensive transportation system which played such an important role in the economic development of the country.

Pass under a bridge. Further on, there is a lane on the left which runs parallel with the canal. Keep along the towpath and pass under a road bridge, after which the canal gradually winds. Shortly, the tower of Acton church can be seen, sitting on elevated ground over to the right. Arrive at bridge 93.

The tomb of Albert Hornby, England's cricket captain during the 1882 Test Match against Australia which gave birth to The Ashes.

6. Leave the towpath and walk over bridge 93. Go through a gate to follow a well-defined path along a field edge. Pass through a gate close to bungalows and follow a hedged-in path to emerge at a bend in a road. Turn right and follow the roadside pavement past dwellings to a crossing road. You are now back in the village of Acton. Turn left and pass the parish hall to return to the car park.

PLACES OF INTEREST

Lying just off the A534 between Acton and Nantwich is magnificent *Dorfold Hall*. The Jacobean exterior has survived the ravages of time and the interior is also in a fine state of repair. The Hall is set amidst attractive gardens which are a delight during the summer months. The Hall and gardens are open on Tuesdays and Bank Holiday Mondays from April to October, between 2 pm and 5 pm.

THE SHROPSHIRE UNION CANAL AT WRENBURY

The walk, apart from presenting an opportunity to survey the village of Wrenbury, also takes in the delightful village of Marbury, which is reached along a cross-country path. From Marbury, a lane gives access to the towpath of the Llangollen Branch of the Shropshire Union Canal for the return journey to Wrenbury.

The Dusty Miller inn by the Shropshire Union Canal.

Wrenbury is a most attractive village and possesses a three-cornered green surrounded by houses, all of which have neat, well-tended gardens. Close by stands the fine 16th-century St Margaret's church which contains a monument dedicated to the memory of Sir Stapleton Cotton, who was a friend and fellow soldier of Wellington. He played a leading part in the victory of Salamanca, for which he was made a viscount, taking the name Combermere, from his family house, Combermere Abbey, which is to the south of Wrenbury. The church also contains some interesting box pews whilst outside there are a number of rather grotesque gargoyles.

The village is a well-known stopping place for holidaymakers using their hired boats on the Llangollen Branch of the Shropshire Union Canal – which winds its way around the outskirts of the village.

The Dusty Miller inn enjoys an idyllic location by the waters of the canal. Formerly a working mill dating back to the 16th century the building was converted into licensed premises in 1977. The inn offers a wide range of bar meals at lunchtime and in the evenings, as well as providing a bistro-style menu. All the meals are home-made and vegetables are steamed, three different types usually being offered with each dish. The inn has a charming 38-seater restaurant on the first floor. There is an extensive canalside beer garden and a garden area for children. Telephone: 01270 780537.

Halfway around the walk, at Marbury, the Swan inn makes an excellent choice for a meal or leisurely drink. Meals are served every lunchtime, except Monday, and every evening.

- HOW TO GET THERE: The A530 connects Nantwich with Whitchurch. The village of Aston, which is about 5 miles from Nantwich, straddles this road. Enter Wrenbury Road and continue through Aston village, passing the Bhurtpore Inn en route; Wrenbury is about one mile further on.

- PARKING: The Dusty Miller inn, which is situated on the north-east side of the village by the Shropshire Union Canal, has a large car park (for patrons). Alternatively, there is roadside parking available close to where the infant river Weaver flows under a lane 180 yards from the inn – reached by crossing the canal over a counter-balanced road bridge.

- LENGTH OF THE WALK: 5½ miles. Map: OS Landranger 117 Chester (GR 590480).

THE WALK

1. From the Dusty Miller inn, follow a lane away from the canal and pass the Cotton Arms to arrive at the green in the centre of the village. The way is to the right here, to enter New Road in the direction of Marbury and Whitchurch, although you may wish to look at the village church before proceeding. After 250 yards pass over the infant river Weaver. Pass a field gate on the right and then leave the lane through the next field gate on the right – where there is a footpath sign.

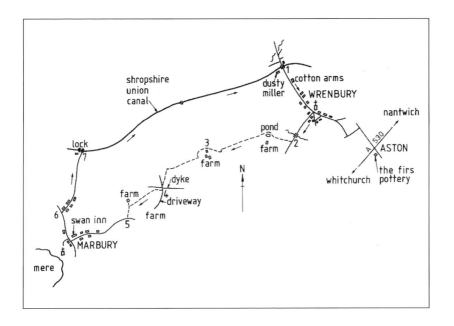

2. With the gate at your back, walk across the facing field, aiming about 80 yards to the right of a farmhouse which can be seen ahead. Keep to the right of a pond which is surrounded by trees and bear slightly left to then go over a stile at the side of a gate. Cross the next field and go over a stile which can be seen about 120 yards away. Follow a track away from the farm. After 150 yards the track finishes. Keep forward now, through a gate, to follow the edge of a large field, keeping a hedgerow on your immediate right. At the field corner turn left and after a further 40 yards go over a stile on the right. Cross a footbridge and immediately go over a second stile. Straight ahead, across a field, there is a farm. Cross the field, aiming to the right of the farm outbuildings.

3. Go over a stile at the side of the outbuildings. There is a fence on the left now. About 60 yards further on, there is a stile which is set in the fence. Go over the stile and bear right to pass through widely planted trees to another stile which can be seen about 80 yards away. Cross the stile and a stream to immediately pass over a second stile which gives access to a field. Turn left and, after only 30 yards, pass over another stile to enter a large field. Turn right and follow the field edge, keeping a hedgerow on your immediate right. A stile at the field

Going through the lock near Marbury.

corner leads to the next field. Turn left and, keeping a row of trees on your immediate left, join a track which leads towards a driveway which can be seen climbing out of a hollow towards a farm on the skyline.

4. On reaching the driveway, which is made of concrete, continue along it and pass over a water-filled dyke. Go through a gate and, about 80 yards further on, leave the driveway over a stile on the right, to enter a large, sloping field. Walk forward, keeping parallel with a fence on the right for 50 yards or so, then bear left and climb up the field to follow the route of overhead power lines. Where the field levels out, keep to the left of bushes to arrive at a stile which is set in a crossing hedgerow about 80 yards to the left of a farmhouse. Cross the stile and turn left to follow the driveway away from the farmhouse. Arrive at a crossing lane, where the way is right.

5. The lane takes you into the village of Marbury. On the right is a fine old inn, the Swan, which overlooks the village green – where a circular seat surrounds an oak tree planted to commemorate the Battle of Waterloo. On passing the inn turn right along Wirswall Road. On the left here, at the side of cottage number 4, is the access lane to the

St Margaret's church in Wrenbury.

village church, which, if time permits, is well worth a visit.

Records show that a church has been here since 1299, although the present building dates from the 15th century. There are many interesting stone carvings around the outside and the church contains an original pulpit which is still in use. Its situation is superb, looking out across the adjacent waters of Marbury Mere.

Having walked past the head of the lane which gives access to the church, arrive at a junction of lanes.

6. Turn right now to enter School Lane, in the direction of Norbury, and keep on past the village hall. Leave the dwellings behind and, after about ¼ mile, arrive at a bridge which carries the lane over a canal – where there is a lock and lock-keeper's cottage.

7. Do not cross the canal but turn right and leave the lane to follow the canal towpath. You are now walking alongside the Llangollen Branch of the Shropshire Union Canal.

The canal was abandoned to navigation in 1944 but was re-opened a few years later following an extensive clearance operation and its route into Wales is an attractive one for the pleasure boaters of today.

Follow the towpath for just over 2 miles, passing under bridge 22 en route, to arrive back at the Dusty Miller inn on the outskirts of Wrenbury village.

PLACES OF INTEREST

The *Firs Pottery* at Aston, which is on Sheppenhall Road close to its junction with the A530 (opposite Wrenbury Road), is an interesting place to visit. The Pottery makes a vast range of functional and decorative pots using stoneware clay which is fired at 1260° in electric and gas kilns. A showroom is attached. Visitors can also spend time actually making their own pottery. Apart from the Pottery, there is a very attractive garden area that visitors are allowed to enjoy, and it is a very pleasant spot in which to relax for a while. Telephone for information: 01270 780345.

THE WEAVER VALLEY AT HANKELOW: ALONG THE SHROPSHIRE UNION CANAL

From the lovely village of Hankelow, the walk takes you along an ancient lane to a footpath which gradually descends into the Weaver valley. A cross-country path then leads to the Shropshire Union Canal for a gentle mile along its towpath before turning for the saunter back to Hankelow, crossing the Weaver once again at the site of Hankelow Mill.

The Shropshire Union Canal

Lying close to the valley of the river Weaver, Hankelow is a most attractive village. The large village green, with its pond and ducks, is overlooked by dwellings old and new. The village can boast a long history. Not very far from the green is Ball Farm, which was built in 1510 and was once the home of Richard Hassall, who was made

Justice of Chester in 1540. Less than a mile from the village is Hankelow Mill, where the waters of the Weaver were used to good effect from the 16th century until recent times when the mill was converted into a private house. To the west of the village, apart from the river Weaver, is the Shropshire Union Canal whose course mirrors that of its un-navigable neighbour between Audlem and Nantwich.

The White Lion inn in the centre of Hankelow is an ideal choice for a meal or a refreshing drink. A Greenalls house, the inn provides a wide variety of food from a sandwich to a fillet steak. Meals can be taken in the restaurant or as bar snacks. There is a pleasantly furnished lounge and a small adjacent beer garden which is popular during warm weather. During 1870 the inn was used as a makeshift court when the preliminary hearing of a murder case was held there prior to a subsequent formal trial at Chester Assizes. Telephone: 01270 811288.

- HOW TO GET THERE: The A529 connects Nantwich with Audlem. The village of Hankelow straddles this road, 1½ miles to the north of Audlem.
- PARKING: There is a car park at the White Lion inn (for patrons). Alternatively, there is a narrow roadside parking area alongside the A529 about ½ mile from the village, in the direction of Audlem, close by the entrance to Corbrook Court (GR 664448). You would then start the walk at point 7.
- LENGTH OF THE WALK: 4½ miles. Map: OS Landranger 118 Stoke-on-Trent. (GR 672454).

THE WALK

1. Enter a macadam lane which commences opposite the White Lion and cross the village green, passing to the right of the duck pond. At the end of the green keep forward along the lane to shortly pass the imposing building of Hankelow Manor. Follow the lane as it turns sharply to the right opposite the entrance to Ball Farm. On the left now is the large black-and-white building of Hankelow Court. The macadam lane terminates where there is a fork of two tracks.

2. Turn left here and go over a stile at the side of a field gate to follow the left hand edge of the field. Over to the right can be seen the red-brick building of Hankelow Hall. A stile to the left of a field gate at the field corner takes you onto a hedged-in path. Emerge from the hedges

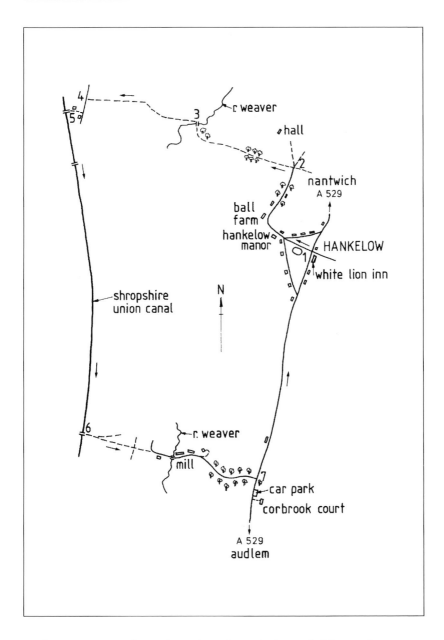

and pass over a stile. Follow the edge of a large field now, keeping a hedgerow on the immediate right. The path takes you onto a track which gently turns to the right. Go over a stile at the side of a gate and

123

The village green at Hankelow.

then, 80 yards further on, cross the infant river Weaver over a flat wooden bridge. Immediately on crossing the river pass through a gate.

3. Turn left now to follow the course of the river but, after only 80 yards, go over a stile at the side of a tree. Climb up the next field to go over a stile in a crossing hedgerow. Keep along the next field where there is a hedge, interspersed with trees, on the immediate left. Go over a stile at the field corner and then bear diagonally right to cross the next field. Arrive at a gate which is set in a barbed-wire fence. Go through the gate and turn left to follow a field edge, keeping the fence on the immediate left. After 80 yards go over a stile at the field corner. Keep forward across the next field to follow a line of widely-spaced trees. On reaching the end of the field go over a stile at the left-hand side of a gateway. Walk along the right hand side of the next field and after 350 yards arrive at the field corner. Go over a stile and plank bridge here, which takes you onto a crossing lane.

4. Turn left along the lane and after 170 yards leave the lane to the right, just before a dwelling is reached, to follow a track. Pass a dwelling and arrive at a bridge. Do not cross the bridge but go through

a gate on the right and descend onto the towpath of the Shropshire Union Canal.

5. Turn left and pass under the bridge, which is number 83. Follow the towpath for one mile, passing under bridge number 82 en route, to arrive at bridge number 80.

Do not walk under this bridge, but leave the towpath here, to climb to a metal gate which gives access to a track.

6. Turn left to follow the track away from the bridge. After 60 yards go over a stile at the left hand side of a gate. The hedge on the right kinks to the right here, where there is a field gate. Go through this gate. Turn left and proceed in the same general direction as before, gradually bearing right, away from a fence on the left. Walk straight over a crossing track via a pair of stiles. Walk forward now along a field edge, keeping a fence on your immediate right. Go over a stile to arrive at a bend in a macadam drive. Keep forward here, in the same direction as before, and then descend past a dwelling. Cross over the infant river Weaver via a bridge and follow a facing lane which takes you past Hankelow Mill (now a private house). A mill has been on this site for hundreds of years and part of the old workings can still be seen down by the riverside.

Continue past The Riverside Mews. There is a dwelling sitting on top of a rise on the left now. Follow the facing lane as it winds and climbs through trees, and after ½ mile emerge onto a crossing road. (The alternative car park near Corbrook Court is a few yards away to the right.)

7. Turn left to follow the roadside verge for 100 yards and then cross the road, taking care, to continue along the roadside pavement.

A gentle stroll takes you back into Hankelow.

PLACES OF INTEREST
Between Nantwich and Audlem, and generally running parallel with the A529, there is a secondary road which connects the A530 near Nantwich with the A525 near Audlem. Directions at both ends of this lane lead to one of Cheshire's more unusual attractions – a secret bunker!

This site, at *Hack Green*, was to have been Cheshire's headquarters in the event of a nuclear war. There are radio rooms, a BBC studio, a decontamination room, two cinemas, a radar museum, a communications centre, military vehicles and a canteen and shop. The bunker is open from 20th March to 31st October between 10.30 am and 5.30 pm every day and also every weekend throughout the winter season and all bank holidays (except Christmas Day and Boxing Day). Telephone: 01270 629219.